Purity of Heart

Is To Will One Thing

Purity of Heart
Is To Will One Thing

*Spiritual Preparation for the Office
of Confession*

by
SØREN KIERKEGAARD

*Translated from the Danish
with an Introductory Essay by*

DOUGLAS V. STEERE
PROFESSOR OF PHILOSOPHY
IN HAVERFORD COLLEGE

HARPER TORCHBOOKS ❧ The Cloister Library

Harper & Row, Publishers
New York

PURITY OF HEART IS TO WILL ONE THING

First HARPER TORCHBOOK edition published 1956

To

"THAT SOLITARY INDIVIDUAL"

this little work is dedicated.

CONTENTS

8 CONTENTS

TRANSLATOR'S INTRODUCTION

WHEN LIFE's weather is fair there are not many who read the Book of *Job* or Pascal's *Thoughts*. Yet in times of outward or inward searching these books seem to many to be the one thing needful and men seek them out.

Søren Kierkegaard is being discovered by the English-speaking world after something over three-quarters of a century of complete neglect. The creative writing of this Danish Pascal was nearly all done in a phenomenally productive six-year period between 1842 and 1848. Kierkegaard died in 1855 at the age of forty-two. The neglect of one who has influenced German theological thought for forty years and who more recently has been openly acknowledged as a formative force upon the minds of such divergent figures as the German philosophers, Karl Jaspers and Martin Heidegger; as Karl Barth; as the lay Catholic thinker, Theodore Haecker, the Jesuit Pryzwara; and as the Spanish philosopher Miguel Unamuno can scarcely be charged to the insularity of the English-speaking religious and philosophical world or to the mere barrier of language. This insularity has been penetrated by far less significant continental and Scandinavian figures, and admirable translations of Scandinavian literature have been available for several decades. A deeper reason must be sought for this Anglo-Saxon neglect and for the present quickening of interest.

The Liberal theologian of England and America is described with commendation by Dean Inge in the closing chapter of his *Types of Christian Saintliness*: "His 'authority' is the best available judgment of civilized humanity which is the Liberal's Great Church. Theological Liberalism is thus a kind of consecration of all the best ethics and science and philosophy regarded as the manifestation or revelation of the will of God to man." This broad, liberal creed supported by a set of idealistic categories that never questioned seriously the progressive revelation of the mind of God in the existing personal and social relationships of man has been too much at home in this prosperous world to need to call out a rebellious Danish religious prophet who challenged the very categories of its thought. But the World War and the condition of soul revealed by the subsequent social, political and economic unsettlements as well as the open contempt for Christianity shown by the new economic and nationalistic religions have forced liberal Christianity to search its very foundations in order to see what is unique in its Christian faith; to ask whether Christianity is simply a synthesis or amalgam of all the finest world thought; to ask where the spring of its dynamic, of its power, of its revolutionary character is to be found; to ask why Christianity is on the defensive, instead of on the offensive; to inquire what the Christian religion demands of a man. It is this mood that is opening the Anglo-Saxon mind of our time to such a radical Christian thinker at Søren Kierkegaard.

Purity of Heart Is to Will One Thing is the first of Kierkegaard's *Edifying Addresses* to be translated into English. It was written in 1846 and was included in the volume of *Edifying Addresses of Varied Tenor* that appeared in Copenhagen on March 13, 1847.

In the two important volumes *Either-Or* and *Stages on Life's Way*, Kierkegaard from 1843 onwards had explored from within the æsthetic and the ethical ways of life, and had done it with an imaginative insight and a dramatic richness scarcely surpassed in the history of literature. Here the æsthetic way of life and the ethical way of life are personified in well-drawn characters and presented in meticulous detail down to their most subtle refinements. Both of these ways of life are shown to be ultimately unstable in one who is aware of their full implications, and to point beyond themselves to the religious way of life, different aspects of which are represented in *Fear and Trembling, Repetition,* the *Concept of Dread, Philosophical Fragments,* and the *Final Unscientific Postscript.*

All of these works were issued not under Kierkegaard's own name but under pseudonyms. They are indirect. They prepare the way. They are intended to unsettle the reader by revealing to him the true character of the dwelling he has inhabited.

But simultaneously with these works, there appeared regularly from 1843 onwards, some twenty *Edifying Addresses,* always bearing Kierkegaard's own name. These are direct. They plunge abruptly into the religious way of life itself and explore it from within.

The title of *Edifying Addresses* (Opbyggelige Taler) sounds quaint and uninviting to the ears of this century. An "address" sounds formal and reminiscent of the days of rhetoric and of ponderous oratory. *Purity of Heart Is to Will One Thing,* like the rest of this series, is really not an address in the ordinary sense at all. It was never spoken aloud to an audience. Like all of Kierkegaard's *Edifying Addresses* which are really unpreached sermons, it was written for men and women to speak aloud to themselves. It was aimed at an audience who read and who pondered what they read. Kierkegaard's own life-long practice of reading sermons aloud to himself convinced him that there was no more effective way to engage with them. In creating these addresses he always spoke them aloud sentence by sentence before he set them down. This may account for the unusual degree of intimate intensity that characterizes them.

The addresses are written to "edify." The Danish word "opbyggelig" means literally "upbuilding," and in spite of the modesty of his prefaces in which he protests that he is without authority and that he makes no pretense of being a teacher, Kierkegaard expressed in his title precisely what he intended for them to do. They were not written as the present-day mind would perhaps prefer them: to entertain, to instruct, or to provoke—but to "upbuild." Yet for Kierkegaard the "upbuilding" of a life could not take place by building on another room like one of the regular additions to a New England farmhouse, or like an interior remodeling that altered a few partitions. No, it was rather an "upbuilding" that called for a costly abandonment of the security of the old under walls. Men must build on a new foundation. They must bottom themselves in a new center. "There are plenty to follow our Lord halfway," declared Meister Eckhart, "but not the other half." The story of the nun, Dame Morel, in the reform of Port Royal, who was ready to give up all of her luxuries but one—all but the key to her little private garden—is the story of men everywhere whom Kierkegaard sought to lay hold of in these *Edifying Addresses*. They wish to keep at least one key back. As Christian swimmers they long to keep one foot on the bottom. Kierkegaard sought to draw them out into water that is 70,000 fathoms deep where life depends not upon half-measures, but upon faith.

These *Edifying Addresses* call for self-examination. They "unconditionally demand the reader's own decisive activity, and all depends on this." They often explore a text and are never troubled if the same text has already been used in several previous addresses. They explore it slowly and deliberately. They look at each facet. Like a spider's web they throw out their main supporting filaments and then from the center outwards they weave around them strand by strand until the web is complete. They would leave no way of escape for one who enters. They would track down evasion into its hidden ways, they would expose every attempt to simulate, they would bring the reader into the very inmost demands of existence within the religious mode. They require patience on the part of the reader, but if he follows them through to their conclusion he can scarcely escape their grip upon his life.

Kierkegaard had a true and realistic respect for the resistance which a man's mind offers to an idea, especially if it is an idea that demands costly action on his part. As a writer he knew how difficult it was to get his own thoughts embodied in suitable words. He suggests that if this is hard, it is ten times as hard to get these words of his to redistil their meaning into the thoughts and into the will of another. He was always ready, therefore, to take infinite pains with what he wrote, and the *Edifying Addresses* were all written over at least three times before they were finally published.

Eduard Geismar, the Danish scholar whose Kierkegaard studies have extended through a life-time, has written of *Purity of Heart Is to Will One Thing*: "It seems to me that nothing that he has written has sprung so directly out of his relationship with God as this address. Anyone who wishes to understand Kierkegaard properly will do well to begin with it."[1] The fact that this address was written as a spiritual preparation for the office of confession does not limit its interest to those who observe church occasions. This office can be celebrated at any moment in the heart of one who is made ready.

Central in the thought of Søren Kierkegaard is his master

[1] Søren Kierkegaard—Eduard Geismar, p. 470. German edition—Vandenhoeck and Ruprecht, Gottingen, 1929.

category *the individual*. All of his thought ultimately had
to pass through the needle's eye of whether or not it compelled men to face their sovereign responsibility as individuals. And this, too, was the pass of Thermopylæ at
which Kierkegaard stationed himself to defend the individual against any philosophical, political, or religious
teaching that tended to slack off this consciousness of the
individual's essential responsibility and integrity.

Purity of Heart Is to Will One Thing, like his other
Edifying Addresses, is directed in the preface to *hiin Enkelte,* "that solitary individual." Yet in this address Kierkegaard succeeds with an exceptional directness in laying
bare what it means to become an individual. The "indirect" method of insinuation which characterizes his approach to this problem in so many of his works is laid
aside here. In one whole section with a relentless persistence
he makes almost a choral refrain of the question, "Do you
live as an individual?"

Kierkegaard apparently intended to attach a much longer
preface to *Purity of Heart Is to Will One Thing* than the
one which appeared there. In this original preface he explained the dedication to *hiin Enkelte* "that solitary individual" and emphasized the importance of this category
of *the individual* to his thought. This important preface
which he later expanded somewhat, was followed by a
second one on the same theme, written in 1847 and 1849,
and by a postscript added in 1855. All three of these
have been preserved and were attached as a supplement
to the posthumously published *The Standpoint of My
Activity as an Author* which appeared in 1859. In these
notes he wrote of the *Edifying Addresses*: "I marked my
writings to which I attached my name with the category
of *the individual* from the beginning; and it continued
like a formula to be repeated in stereotyped fashion so that

the individual is not a later invention of mine but has been there from the beginning."[2]

When Kierkegaard speaks of *hiin Enkelte* in his dedicatory preface, he means more than we do by our words "that individual." The nearest English expression that approaches it is "that solitary individual." He means the individual as separated from the rest, the individual as he would be if he were solitary and alone, face to face with his destiny, with his vocation, with the Eternal, with God Himself who had singled him out.

Perhaps Descartes was on the right road when he sought to isolate the individual *I* in man from all other experience and make it the starting point for his system. But he was wrong and even culpable in not pressing on in his exploration of the *I* beyond its capacity to think, for thought, Kierkegaard would insist, is not its most unique endowment. Here in the core of the *I* is a center from which choice springs, from which responsibility for one's acts springs, from which the ultimate sense of uneasiness and weariness with anything that is short of the highest of all in reality ultimately issues, from which remorse and repentance arises.

Allow this center in a man to remain dulled by the crowd; allow it to continue dissipated by busyness; permit it to go on evading its function by a round of distractions, or to lull itself by a carefully chosen rotation of pleasures, abandon it to its attempt to drug, to narcotize suffering and remorse which might reveal to it its true condition; let it wither away the sense of its own validity by false theories of man's nature, of his place in the social pattern, of his way of salvation; in short, allow any of these well-known forms of domestication of man's responsible core as an individual, to continue unchallenged, and you as a

[2] *Collected Works*, Vol. XIII, p. 605.

thinker and a friend of men have committed the supreme treason!

"In one's friend one shall have one's best enemy," wrote Nietzsche, and in Kierkegaard the reader finds that he is confronted with a merciless enemy to every form of gregarious domestication within himself. Kierkegaard does not risk smothering his reader with leniency. He is prepared to be hard, to wound in order to heal, to use the knife. Kierkegaard conceived it his function as a writer to strip men of their disguises, to compel them to see evasions for what they are, to label blind alleys, to cut off men's retreats, to tear down the niggardly roofs they continue to build over their precious sun-dials, to isolate men from the crowd, to enforce self-examination, and to bring them solitary and alone before the Eternal. Here he left them. For here that in man which makes him a responsible individual must itself act or it must take flight. No other can make this decision. Only when man is alone can he face the Eternal. And the act that is called for at this point is not one of mere noetic recognition. When all is known that can be known, the responsible core of the will in the man has still to yield. He must act, he must choose, he must risk, he must make the leap. For in an existence where qualitative differences remain, there is no other entry into the deepest level of existential living as an individual. Only by this leap on faith could one know the release of guilt, the sense of commitment, the acceptance of a vocation, of a calling in whose service is perfect freedom. For in any lesser service there is servility. Only the Omnipotent One dares exercise that restraint of true love that makes its associates free and heightens, not debases, the individual core of responsibility and integrity within them. "The consciousness of one's eternal responsibility to be an individual is the one thing needful."

Only in the light of this his central task can Kierkegaard's attacks upon the philosophical speculation of Hegel or upon the social, political and ecclesiastical life of his day be understood. Hegel tended always to make the individual a mere passing-point, a moment, in the cosmic process, and to insist on the individual's gaining his concrete ethical significance through being identified with the social, religious, and political institutions of his time. Man is to be saved by identification with a set of external arrangements. This for Kierkegaard is the ultimate blasphemy. For instead of heightening his core of responsibility and integrity man is invited to do what he is already enamored with doing, to join the crowd, the mass, to be dissolved into the organic whole. To become a set of relations within the whole is all too congenial to modern man, Kierkegaard believed. "It must be apparent to anyone with even a little dialectical skill, that one cannot attack the (Hegelian) system from within. Outside of it, however, there is only one free seminal point 'the individual,' ethically, religiously, and existentially accentuated."[3] It was with this creative category of *the individual* that Kierkegaard attacked the Hegelian system.

All of these changes of outer arrangements, whether they be ecclesiastical, social, or political, seemed to Kierkegaard to gloss over the real problem—which was the awakening of *the individual*. Hence his profound disappointment in Luther's having allowed himself to be lured eventually into a mere rebellion against the Pope, a casting off the yoke of the monastic system and of ascetic practices, instead of laying on men the even costlier responsibility of their vocation before God. The inward reformation was yet to come. Kierkegaard believed himself to be its prophet. Here, too, was rooted his disappointment and impatience

[3] *Ibid.*, p. 604.

with the social revolutions of 1848 that believed by an
upheaval of mass external arrangements to be able to re-
solve the basic problem of men. "In the future each effort
at reformation, if its leader be a true reformer, will direct
itself against the mass as such and not against the government," he wrote in his *Journal* amid the rumblings of
1847. Such an attempt as Tolstoy's to find inwardness by
becoming poor with the poor, or Lenin's utopian endeavor
to usher in a kind of social salvation by making all of the
proletariat rich would only have met with Kierkegaard's
contempt. For they still rely on outer arrangements, they
are still concerned primarily with "housekeeping," and
the deeper problem is left untouched.

The effort of Gruntvig and his school to whip up the
national pride of Denmark by recalling it to the Nordic
sagas and its glorious history, Kierkegaard felt to be so
much public flattery and a violent poison to the real individual need of the soul. The comfortable Danish church in
general he found to be blind to its compromises with bour-
geois life which had reduced it to a low-pressure form of
Christianity. This church stood out for him in sharpest
contrast to the primitive Christian community.

All attempts at mass prescription, all things attainable
in the mass as such, in fact the very notion of the crowd,
of the mass, drew the most violent invective Kierkegaard
had at his command. For he believed the crowd, the mass,
to be a hiding-place in which the individual may abdi-
cate his true quest for inward intensity and responsibility.
The crowd is a sink of cowardice in which individuals are
relieved of individual responsibility and will commit acts
they would never dare to do alone. When a man is to be
executed by shooting, not one executioner shoots, but several. When the noble Caius Marius was seized, no individual
soldier dared touch him, but a crowd of them had no

such restraint. "Take the highest of all, think of Christ—
and think of the whole human race, all that have been
born and will be born. Now the situation is one where
Christ is alone, so that someone as an individual alone
with Christ stepped up to Him and spat upon Him: the
man was never born and will never be born, who possesses
the courage or the audacity to do this: that is the truth.
As they became a crowd, however, they had the courage
to do it—oh, terrible falsity."[4] The mass flatters, the mass
excuses, the mass condemns, the mass counts heads, the
mass pronounces on truth, and in all these things the mass,
for Kierkegaard, is that which is both false and debasing.
To speak of *social salvation,* of salvation by group, by
tribe, by race, by class, by nation, is for Kierkegaard an
act of spiritual betrayal.

This isolation of man from the flock, from the mass,
from the crowd and the heightening of his consciousness
as an individual which the Eternal accomplishes is a central theme of *Purity of Heart Is to Will One Thing.*
Before the quiet gaze of the Eternal, there is no hiding-
place. As individuals we are what we are before God, and
no mass opinion affects this in the least. Kierkegaard believed that his generation was seeking to live in mere time
and to make the Eternal superfluous. He reminded them of
the Eternal's power to dissolve away time and to separate
the crowd into individuals. In memory, in conscience, in
remorse, in work at a calling, in the solitude, the Eternal
still impinges upon the individual and awakens him to a
consciousness both of himself and of his responsibility and
of his worth to the Eternal.

In this polemic against the mass, the crowd, Kierkegaard
could never be justly accused of parading a new snobbish
aristocracy, a small upper-house of supermen. "The reader

4 *Ibid.,* p. 594.

will consider that here *the mass* is not . . . a *common herd*.
God in heaven, what if the religious way should fall into
such an inhuman division of mankind! No, the *mass* is a
number, the numerical. A number of the nobility, the
millionaires, the highest dignitaries, etc., can through the
use of the numerical quite as readily become the *mass*."[5]
"It is 'the mass'—not this one or that one—that is now
living, now dead, not a group of menials or of aristocrats,
of rich or of poor, but the mass understood in a purely
conceptual sense—which is the false. For as a man is in
a crowd, he is released from repentance and responsibility
or at least is weakened in responsibility for himself as an
individual."[6] Again in his *Journal* for 1847 he wrote, "I
long to call the attention of the mass to its own doom."

In the world, the native differences of gifts in men are
obvious. And in this world the drift toward perpetuating
these inequalities by one form of aristocracy or another is
powerful. Kierkegaard saw only one solvent for these obvious inequalities, only one root of enduring equality between all men. That equality is in the equality of concern
which a loving Eternal Father has for each individual that
has ever existed. Hence only in the Christian sense of
being children of a common Father are we all equal. To
those impatient political enthusiasts who talk loudly on
how futile and impractical religion must always be, and
who are bent on legislating human equality into existence,
Kierkegaard offers a word of counsel, "Only that which
is religious can with the assistance of eternity press the
equality of men through to its ultimate conclusions: the
reverent, genuine, unworldly, true, the only possible equality between men. And therefore that which is religious,

[5] *Collected Works*, Vol. XIII, p. 593.
[6] *Ibid.*, pp. 593-594.

may it be said to its glorification, is also the true humanity."[7]

In his brief essay on the *Difference between a Genius and an Apostle* he returns to this theme. The genius, an aristocrat of the spirit, has had gifts lavished upon him by nature that distinguish him from his fellows. The apostle may be a commoner, a fisherman, a one-talent man by nature, or he may have ten talents—yet all that he has is dedicated to the service of the Eternal and as such is lifted up. The genius speaks with brilliance and charm. The apostle speaks with authority. The way of the genius is a way closed to all but a few. The way of the apostle is a way open to all as individuals—even to the genius himself if he can forsake the absorbing satisfactions of a brilliant self-sufficiency and be ready to will one thing. Kierkegaard knew himself as only a genius, only an aristocrat of the spirit. He would never style himself an apostle or claim to speak with authority. God alone could judge of that, God before whom all men irrespective of their talents are really equal.

The root of equality is therefore grounded in this unchanging personal relation between the individual and God, not in the secular whim or political fashion of the crowd. Here, too, in the personal concrete particular category of the *individual* as opposed to the mechanical abstract impersonal category of the crowd or the mass, Kierkegaard found the root of enduring neighbor-love. There is nothing in Holy Scripture, he points out, about loving man in the mass—only about loving your neighbor as yourself. For then you separate him out of the abstract mass or public, and he becomes an individual. And when you love him as yourself you testify to that deep equality of all men as individuals before God. And you do it *per-*

[7] *Ibid.,* p. 590.

sonally. "That one shall honor each individual man, without exception, each man: that is truth and is reverence and is neighbor-love."[8]

Little needs be added here to what has already been written in English about the bare facts of Kierkegaard's life. He was a sufferer. The melancholy shade of his father's closely held sin, the breaking of his engagement with Regina Olsen, the public ridicule to which his sensitive nature was exposed by the public attack of the modish Copenhagen journal *Corsair*, the disillusionment with Bishop Mynster and the church in his closing years, all bore in upon him. What is significant about Kierkegaard is the use he made of this suffering. He refused to seek invulnerability. He accepted the suffering, he lived with it, he searched it, and he found its costly meaning for him—that he was to live as one called under God—to live as a lonely man—to live for an idea. Through suffering he found, and later was kept in his vocation. For his intense nature this pressure of suffering meant debauchery, insanity, suicide—or the penetration of the sorrow for its message. A *Journal* entry in 1843 reads, "The most important thing of all is that a man stands right toward God, does not try to wrench away from something, but rather penetrates it until it yields its explanation. Whether or not it turns out as he wishes; it is still the best of all."

Seldom in the history of literature has there been seen such productivity as was released in him between the years of 1842 and 1848. In the single year 1843, he published in February, his long *Either-Or*; in May, *Two Edifying Addresses*; in October, three of his works *Fear and Trembling*, *The Repetition* and *Three Edifying Addresses* appeared on the same day; and in December, a further volume of *Four Edifying Addresses*.

[8] *Ibid.*, p. 597. This is also the theme of his *Works of Love.*

He found in his writing a form of worship of God, and in the exercise of his calling as a writer whose every page was composed as under the scrutiny of God, he found his healing. If one is as weak as he is, and has so much to do, he will soon learn what it is to pray, he suggests. And he describes his vocation as a writer as literally living with God as one lives with a Father. He rises in the morning and gives thanks to God. Then work begins. At a set time in the evening, he breaks off and again gives thanks to God. Then sleep. So he lives. The twelve-hour day of writing when his production was at its height is broken only by a midday walk among the common people in the Østergade. This keeping of sorrow and remorse silently between oneself and God keeps a man humble and acutely aware of the service he owes to God. Buried in this center, these sufferings release light that has no fear of darkness. And rarely in religious literature has suffering been treated with such delicacy and penetration as in Kierkegaard's own writings.

His vocation, his calling, is not your calling. No one could be more faithful than Kierkegaard in pointing that out. But do you know what is your calling, what is your vocation, and have you accepted it? It is these questions that he asks again and again in the closing sections of *Purity of Heart Is to Will One Thing*.

In his *Journals* he makes a comment on the function of an introduction to a book. It should serve to unclothe the spectators from their diverse preoccupations and get them ready for the real bath. Kierkegaard's own brief preface to *Purity of Heart Is to Will One Thing* does little more than begin this process, and tempts me to suggest that one who is not familiar with other works of Kierkegaard, will find himself still better prepared for immersion in this address if he turns immediately to Section Twelve and reads from that point to the end. By the use of a brilliant analogy this twelfth section begins by describing the true and the false way of reading or listening to a devotional address and the following sections set forth with pointed directness the central issue of what it means to be an individual. After reading this, the address should then be read through from beginning to end, read "willingly and slowly," read "over and over again," and given "the reader's own decisive activity, and all depends on this."

The translator wishes to express his thanks to Professor Eduard Geismar for suggesting the undertaking of this work; to Professor C. C. J. Webb and Hanna Astrup Larsen for corrections and suggested improvements in the translation. The translation and notes are made from the eighth volume of the standard Danish edition of Kierkegaard's *Collected Works* edited by A. B. Drachmann, J. L. Heiberg, and H. O. Lange and published by the Gyldendalske Boghandel, Copenhagen, 1903-06. The fifteen sectional divisions and headings have been supplied by the translator.

DOUGLAS V. STEERE

HAVERFORD, PENNSYLVANIA.
March, 1938.

TRANSLATOR'S NOTE
to the Revised Edition
of the English Translation

THIS TRANSLATION into English of Kierkegaard's *Purity of Heart* was made in 1935 and first published in 1938. It was one of the first translations of Kierkegaard to appear in English and it took no small amount of courage on Harper & Brothers' part to put it into print. Since that time nearly all of Kierkegaard's works except his voluminous journals have been translated, and the influence of his thought has made itself widely felt in both England and America. Before a fourth printing of *Purity of Heart* was to appear, it seemed right to make a very thorough re-examination of the translation from the Danish in order to correct certain errors and misprints and in places to improve the form of expression. I am deeply indebted to my dear friend, Howard T. Lutz, for his invaluable assistance at every point in this revision, although the responsibility for changes and for the final text is of course my own.

After having introduced many persons and groups to Kierkegaard during the past fifteen years, I am still of Professor Eduard Geismar's opinion that there is no better way to begin to grasp Kierkegaard's religious message than to read *Purity of Heart*. I should then follow it by *Training in Christianity* and by the excellent *Selections from the Journals* translated by Alexander Dru.

As a devotional classic, the nineteenth century produced almost nothing in either Catholic or Protestant circles that can compare seriously with *Purity of Heart*. Designed as a preparation for the church's office of confession, it is prepared to put into the hands of the serious reader the surgical instruments for a major spiritual operation. The instruments are razor-sharp and they can cut through any cancerous worldly growth, no matter how fibrous, in order to liberate again the healthy tissues of a man's individual responsibility before the gaze of the living God.

The note that it sounds is alien to the modern ears which are tuned to collective thinking, collective action and collective salvation. It is, however, not an individualistic nineteenth-century note that Kierkegaard sounds, but a universal note of the inward life of man, a note that even this age will be compelled to learn again when its present grim honeymoon with collective salvation has spent itself.

Already there are many whose spiritual needs are so acute that they are open for such direction as this book provides. Already there are those who do not merely want help against the symptoms, who do not want some swift short-cut to "peace of mind," but who can stand a ruthlessly accurate diagnosis of the disease that has produced the symptoms, and can bear to read of a remedy so costly that it can only be begun but not concluded in this life. To these persons *Purity of Heart* will continue to minister and to minister faithfully.

DOUGLAS V. STEERE

January 20, 1948.

PREFACE

ALTHOUGH THIS little book (it can be called an occasional address, yet without having the occasion which produces the speaker and gives him authority, or the occasion which produces the reader and makes him eager to learn) is like a fantasy, like a dream by day as it confronts the relationships of actuality: yet it is not without assurance and not without hope of accomplishing its object. It is in search of that solitary "individual," to whom it wholly abandons itself, by whom it wishes to be received as if it had arisen within his own heart; that solitary "individual" whom with joy and gratitude I call my reader; that solitary "individual" who reads willingly and slowly, who reads over and over again, and who reads aloud—for his own sake. If it finds him, then in the distance of the separation the understanding is perfect, if he retains for himself both the distance and the understanding in the inwardness of appropriation.

When a woman makes an altar cloth, so far as she is able, she makes every flower as lovely as the graceful flowers of the field, as far as she is able, every star as sparkling as the glistening stars of the night. She withholds nothing, but uses the most precious things she possesses. She sells off every other claim upon her life that she may purchase the most uninterrupted and favorable time of the day and night for her one and only, for her beloved work. But when the cloth is finished and put to its sacred use: then she is deeply distressed if someone should make the mistake of looking at her art, instead of at the meaning of the cloth; or make the mistake of looking at a defect, instead of at the meaning of the cloth. For she could not work

27

the sacred meaning into the cloth itself, nor could she sew it on the cloth as though it were one more ornament. This meaning really lies in the beholder and in the beholder's understanding, if he, in the endless distance of the separation, above himself and above his own self, has completely forgotten the needlewoman and what was hers to do. It was allowable, it was proper, it was duty, it was a precious duty, it was the highest happiness of all for the needlewoman to do everything in order to accomplish what was hers to do; but it was a trespass against God, an insulting misunderstanding of the poor needlewoman, when someone looked wrongly and saw what was only there, not to attract attention to itself, but rather so that its omission would not distract by drawing attention to itself.

                                                              S.K.

Purity of Heart

Is To Will One Thing

1. Introduction:
Man and the Eternal

FATHER IN HEAVEN! What is a man without Thee! What is all that he knows, vast accumulation though it be, but a chipped fragment if he does not know Thee! What is all his striving, could it even encompass a world, but a half-finished work if he does not know Thee: Thee the One, who art one thing and who art all! So may Thou give to the intellect, wisdom to comprehend that one thing; to the heart, sincerity to receive this understanding; to the will, purity that wills only one thing. In prosperity may Thou grant perseverance to will one thing; amid distractions, collectedness to will one thing; in suffering, patience to will one thing. Oh, Thou that giveth both the beginning and the completion, may Thou early, at the dawn of day, give to the young man the resolution to will one thing. As the day wanes, may Thou give to the old man a renewed remembrance of his first resolution, that the first may be like the last, the last like the first, in possession of a life that has willed only one thing. Alas, but this has indeed not come to pass. Something has come in between. The separation of sin lies in between. Each day, and day after day something is being placed in between: delay, blockage, interruption, delusion, corruption. So in this time of repentance may Thou give the courage once again to will one thing. True, it is an interruption of our ordinary tasks; we do lay down our work as though it were a day of rest, when the penitent (and it is only in a time of repentance that the heavy-laden worker may be quiet in the confession of sin) is alone before Thee in self-accusation. This is in-

31

deed an interruption. But it is an interruption that searches back into its very beginnings that it might bind up anew that which sin has separated, that in its grief it might atone for lost time, that in its anxiety it might bring to completion that which lies before it. Oh, Thou that givest both the beginning and the completion, give Thou victory in the day of need so that what neither a man's burning wish nor his determined resolution may attain to, may be granted unto him in the sorrowing of repentance: to will only one thing.

"To everything there is a season," says Solomon.[1] And in these words he voices the experience of the past and of that which lies behind us. For when an old man relives his life, he lives it only by dwelling upon his memories; and when wisdom in an old man has outgrown the immediate impressions of life, the past viewed from the quiet of memory is something different from the present in all its bustle. The time of work and of strain, of merrymaking and of dancing is over. Life requires nothing more of the old man and he claims nothing more of it. By being present, one thing is no nearer to him than another. Expectation, decision, repentance in regard to a thing do not affect his judgment. By being a part of the past, these distinctions all become meaningless, for that which is completely past has no present to which it may attach itself. Oh, the desolation of old age, if to be an old man means this: means that at any given moment a living person could look at life as if he himself did not exist, as if life were merely a past event that held no more present tasks for him as a living person, as if he, as a living person, and life were cut off from each other within life, so that life was past and gone, and he had become a stranger to it. Oh, tragic wisdom, if it were of everything human that Solomon spoke, and if

IS TO WILL ONE THING

the speech must ever end in the same manner, insisting
that everything has its time, in the well-known words:
"What profit hath he that worketh in that wherein he
laboureth" (Ecclesiastes 3:9)? Perhaps the meaning would
have been clearer if Solomon had said, "There was a time
for all, all had its time," in order to show that, as an old
man, he is speaking of the past and that in fact he is not
speaking to someone but is talking to himself. For the
person who talks about human life, which changes with
the years, must be careful to state his own age to his
listeners. And that wisdom which is related to such a
changeable and temporal element in a man must, as with
every frailty, be treated with caution in order that it shall
not work harm.

Only the Eternal is always appropriate and always present, is always true. Only the Eternal applies to each human
being, whatever his age may be. The changeable exists, and
when its time has passed it is changed. Therefore any statement about it is subject to change. That which may be
wisdom when spoken by an old man about past events may
be folly in the mouth of a youth or of a grown man when
spoken of the present. The youth would not be able to
understand it and the grown man would not want to
understand it. Even one who is a little advanced in age may
fully agree with Solomon in saying, "There is a time to
dance from sheer joy." And yet how can he agree with him?
For his dancing time is past, and therefore he speaks of it
as of something past. And it does not matter whether, in
that day when both youth and the longing to dance were
his, he grieved at its being denied him, or whether in joyous
abandon he yielded to the invitation to dance: one who is
a little advanced in age will still say quietly, "There is a
time to dance." But for the youth, to be allowed to hurry
off to the dance and to sit shut in at home are two such

different things that it does not occur to him to consider them on the same level and to say, "There is a time for the one and a time for the other." A man is changed in the course of the years, and each time some portion of life lies behind him he tends to talk of its varied content as if it were all on the same level. But it does not follow from this that he has become any wiser. For by this, one has only said that he has changed. Perhaps even now there is something that makes him restless in the same way that the dance disturbs the youth, something that absorbs his attention in the same way that a toy absorbs a child. It is in this manner that a man changes, over the years. Old age is the final change. The old man speaks in the same vein of it all, of all the changeable that is now past.

But is this all of the story? Has all been heard that may be said about being a man, and about man's temporal life? The most important and decisive thing of all is certainly left out. For the talk about the natural changes of human life over the years, together with what externally happened there, is not in essence any different from talking of plant or of animal life. The animal also changes with the years. When it is older it has other desires than it had at an earlier age. At certain times it, too, has its happiness in life, and at other times it must endure hardship. Yes, when late autumn comes, even the flower can speak the wisdom of the years and say with truthfulness, "All has its time, there is 'a time to be born and a time to die'; there is a time to jest lightheartedly in the spring breeze, and a time to break under the autumn storm; there is a time to burst forth into blossom, beside the running water, beloved by the stream, and a time to wither and be forgotten; a time to be sought out for one's beauty, and a time to be unnoticed in one's wretchedness; there is a time to be nursed with care, and a time to be cast out with contempt;

there is a time to delight in the warmth of the morning sun and a time to perish in the night's cold. All has its time; 'what profit hath he that worketh in that wherein he laboureth?' "

Yes, the animal, too, when it has lived its time may speak the wisdom of the years and say with truth, "All has its time. There is a time to leap with joy, and a time to drag oneself along the earth; there is a time to waken early, and a time to sleep long; there is a time to run with the herd, and a time to go apart to die; there is a time to build nests with one's beloved, and there is a time to sit alone on the roof; there is a time to soar freely among the clouds, and a time to sink heavily to the earth. All has its time; 'what profit hath he that worketh in that wherein he laboureth?' " And, in case you should say to the flower, "Is there, then, nothing more to tell?" then it will answer you, "No, when the flower is dead, the story is over." Otherwise the story must have been different from the beginning and been different as it went along, not merely becoming different at the end. For let us assume that the flower concluded its story in another fashion and added, "The story is not over, for when I am dead, I am immortal." Would this not be a strange story? If the flower were really immortal then immortality must be just that which prevented it from dying, and therefore immortality must have been present in each instant of its life. And the story of its life must once again have been wholly different in order to express continually immortality's difference from all the changeableness and the different kinds of variations of the perishable. Immortality cannot be a final alteration that crept in, so to speak, at the moment of death as the final stage. On the contrary, it is a changelessness that is not altered by the passage of the years. Therefore, to the old man's words that "all has its time," the wise Solomon adds, "God made all things beautiful in his time; also he hath set eternity within man's heart" (Ecclesiastes 3:11).[2] Thus says the sage. For the talk about change, and the varied way of talking about change is indeed confusing, even when it comes from the mouth of an old man. Only the Eternal is constructive. The wisdom of the years is confusing. Only the wisdom of eternity is edifying.

If there is, then, something eternal in a man, it must be able to exist and to be grasped within every change. Nor can it be wisdom to say, indiscriminately, that this something eternal has its time like the perishable, that it makes its circle like the wind that never gets further; that it has its course like the river that never fills up the sea. Nor can it be wisdom to talk of this eternal element in the same vein as if one were speaking of the past, as if it is past and past in the sense that it can never, not even in repentance, relate itself to a present person but only to an absent one. For repentance is precisely the relation between something past and someone that has his life in the present time. It was unwise of the youth to wish to talk in the same terms of the pleasure of dancing and of its opposite. For this clear act of folly betrayed that the youth, in his youth, would like to have outgrown youth. But as for the Eternal, the time never comes when a man has grown away from it, or has become older—than the Eternal.

If there is, then, something eternal in a man the discussion of it must have a different ring. It must be said that there is something that shall always have its time, something that a man shall always do, just as one Apostle says that we should always give thanks to God.[3] For that which has its time must properly be looked upon as an associate and an equal with other temporal things that in their turn shall pass away. But the Eternal is that which is set over all. The Eternal will not have its time, but will fashion time to its own desire, and then give its consent that the temporal should also be given its time. So the Scripture says, "The one shall be done, the other shall not be neglected."[4] But that which shall not be neglected is just that which cannot come into consideration until that is done which ought to be done. In like fashion with the Eternal. If the wisdom of life should ever alter that which concerns the eternal in a man to the point of changing it into something temporal, then this would be folly whether it be spoken by an old man or by a youth. For in relation to the Eternal, age gives no justification for speaking absurdly, and youth does not exclude one from being able to grasp what is true. Should someone explain that the fear of God, in the sense of that felt in this world of time, should belong to childhood and therefore disappear with the years as does childhood itself, or should be like a happy state of mind that cannot be maintained, but only remembered; should someone explain that penitence comes like the weakness of old age, with the wasting away of strength, when the senses are blunted, when sleep no longer strengthens but weakens; then this would be impiety and folly. Yes, to be sure, it is a fact that there was a man who with the years forgot his childish fear of God, was swindled out of the best, and was taken in by that which was most insolent. Yes, to be sure, it is a fact that there was a man whom repentance first overtook in the painfulness of old age, when he no longer had the strength to sin, so that the repentance not only came late, but the despair of late repentance became the final stage. But this is no story of an event that calls for an ingenious explanation or that would even of itself explain life. When it happens, it is a horrible thing. And even if a man should become a thousand years old, he would not have become

so old that he dares speak otherwise of it than the youth
—with fear and trembling. For in relation to the Eternal,
a man ages neither in the sense of time nor in the sense
of an accumulation of past events. No, when an old person
has outgrown the childish and the youthful, ordinary language calls this, maturity and a gain. But willfully ever
to have outgrown the Eternal is spoken of as falling away
from God and as perdition; and only the life of the
ungodly "shall be as the snail that melts, as it goes"
(Psalm 58:8).

2. Remorse, Repentance, Confession:
Eternity's Emissaries to Man

THERE IS, then, something which should at all
times be done. There is something which in no temporal
sense shall have its time. Alas, and when this is not done,
when it is omitted, or when just the opposite is done, then
once again, there is something (or more correctly it is
the same thing, that reappears, changed, but not changed
in its essence) which should at all times be done. There
is something which in no temporal sense shall have its
time. There must be repentance and remorse.

One dare not say of repentance and remorse that it has
its time; that there is a time to be carefree and a time to
be prostrated in repentance. Such talk would be: to the
anxious urgency of repentance—unpardonably slow; to
the grieving after God—sacrilege; to what should be done
this very day, in this instant, in this moment of danger—
senseless delay. For there is indeed danger. There is a dan-

ger that is called delusion. It is unable to check itself. It goes on and on: then it is called perdition. But there is a concerned guide, a knowing one, who attracts the attention of the wanderer, who calls out to him that he should take care. That guide is remorse. He is not so quick of foot as the indulgent imagination, which is the servant of desire. He is not so strongly built as the victorious intention. He comes on slowly afterwards. He grieves. But he is a sincere and faithful friend. If that guide's voice is never heard, then it is just because one is wandering along the way of perdition. For when the sick man who is wasting away from consumption believes himself to be in the best of health, his disease is at the most terrible point. If there were some one who early in life steeled his mind against all remorse and who actually carried it out, nevertheless remorse would come again if he were willing to repent even of this decision. So wonderful a power is remorse, so sincere is its friendship that to escape it entirely is the most terrible thing of all. A man can wish to slink away from many things in life, and he may even succeed, so that life's favored one can say in the last moment, "I slipped away from all the cares under which other men suffered." But if such a person wishes to bluster out of, to defy, or to slink away from remorse, alas, which is indeed the most terrible to say of him, that he failed, or—that he succeeded?

A Providence watches over each man's wandering through life. It provides him with two guides. The one calls him forward. The other calls him back. They are, however, not in opposition to each other, these two guides, nor do they leave the wanderer standing there in doubt, confused by the double call. Rather the two are in eternal understanding with each other. For the one beckons forward to the Good, the other calls man back from evil. Nor are they blind guides. Just for that reason there are two of them. For in order to make the journey secure, they must look both forward and backward. Alas, there was perhaps many a one who went astray through not understanding how to continue a good beginning. For his course was along a false way, and he pressed on so continuously that remorse could not call him back onto the old way. There was perhaps someone who went astray because, in the exhaustion of repentance, he could go no further, so that the guide could not help him to find the way forward. When a long procession is about to move, a call is heard first from the one who is furthest forward. But he waits until the last has answered. The two guides call out to a man early and late, and when he listens to their call, then he finds his way, then he can know where he is, on the way. Because these two calls designate the place and show the way. Of these two, the call of remorse is perhaps the best. For the eager traveler who travels lightly along the way does not, in this fashion, learn to know it as well as a wayfarer with a heavy burden. The one who merely strives to get on does not learn to know the way as well as the remorseful man. The eager traveler hurries forward to the new, to the novel, and, indeed, away from experience. But the remorseful one, who comes behind, laboriously gathers up experience.

The two guides call out to a man early and late. And yet, no, for when remorse calls to a man it is always late. The call to find the way again by seeking out God in the confession of sins is always at the eleventh hour. Whether you are young or old, whether you have sinned much or little, whether you have offended much or neglected much, the guilt makes this call come at the eleventh hour. The inner agitation of the heart understands what remorse insists upon, that the eleventh hour has come. For in the sense of time, the old man's age is the eleventh

hour; and the instant of death, the final moment in the
eleventh hour. The indolent youth speaks of a long life
that lies before him. The indolent old man hopes that his
death is still a long way off. But repentance and remorse
belong to the eternal in a man. And in this way each time
that repentance comprehends guilt it understands that the
eleventh hour has come: that hour which human indolence knows well enough exists and will come, when
it is talked about in generalities, but not when it actually
applies to the indolent one himself. For even the old man
thinks that there is some time left and the indolent youth
deceives himself when he thinks that difference in age is
the determining factor in regard to the nearness of the
eleventh hour. See, then, how good and how necessary it
is that there are two guides. For whether it be the lightly
armed desire of youth which it is presumed will press
forward to victory, or whether it be the mature man's
determination that will fight its way through life, they
both count on having a long time at their disposal. They
presuppose, in the plans for their efforts, a generation or
at least a number of years, and therefore they waste a
great deal of time and on that account the whole thing
so readily ends in delusion.

But repentance and remorse know how to make use
of time in fear and trembling. When remorse awakens
concern, whether it be in the youth, or in the old man,
it awakens it always at the eleventh hour. It does not have
much time at its disposal, for it is at the eleventh hour.
It is not deceived by a false notion of a long life, for it
is at the eleventh hour. And in the eleventh hour one
understands life in a wholly different way than in the
days of youth or in the busy time of manhood or in the
final moment of old age. He who repents at any other
hour of the day repents in the temporal sense. He fortifies
himself by a false and hasty conception of the insignifi-

cance of his guilt. He braces himself with a false and hasty notion of life's length. His remorse is not in true inwardness of spirit. Oh, eleventh hour, wherever thou art present, how all is changed! How still everything is, as if it were the midnight hour; how sober, as if it were the hour of death; how lonely, as if it were among the tombs; how solemn, as if it were within eternity. Oh, heavy hour of labor (although labor is at rest), when the account is rendered, yet there is no accuser there; when all is called by its own name, yet there is nothing said; when each improper word must be repeated, in the light of eternity! Oh, costly bargain, where remorse must pay so dearly for what seemed in the eyes of lightheartedness and busyness and proud struggling and impatient passion and the judgment of the world to be reckoned as nothing! Oh, eleventh hour, how terrible if Thou shouldst remain, how much more terrible than if death should continue through a whole life!

So repentance must have its time if all is not to be confused. For there are two guides. The one beckons forward. The other calls back. But repentance shall not have its time in a temporal sense. It will not belong to a certain section of life as fun and play belong to childhood, or as the excitement of love belongs to youth. It will not come and disappear as a whim or as a surprise. No, remorse should be an action with a collected mind, so that it may be spoken of to the edification of the hearer and so that new life may be born of it, so that it does not become an event whose sorrowful heritage is a feeling of sadness. In a setting of freedom, bearing the impress of eternity, repentance should have its time, yes, even its time of preparation. For in proportion to what should be done there, the time of collection and preparation is not a drawn-out affair. On the contrary there is a sense of reverence, a holy fear, a humility, that that which is to be done in the pure sincerity of this act of repentance may not become vain and overhasty. That a man wishes to prepare himself is no torpid delay. On the contrary, it is an intense agitation of heart that is already in alliance with what is to be done there. From the point of view of the Eternal, repentance must come instantaneously, indeed there is not even time to utter the words. But man is in the temporal dimension and moves along in time. Thus the Eternal and the temporal seek to make themselves intelligible to each other. Just as the temporal does not wish for delay simply in order to withdraw itself, but, conscious of its weakness, asks time to prepare itself; so the Eternal yields not because it gives up its claim, but in order by tender treatment to give frail man a little time.

The Eternal with its "obey at once" must not become a sudden shock which merely confuses the temporal. It should, on the contrary, be of assistance to the temporal throughout life. As the superior in relation to its mental inferior, or as an older person in relation to a child, can press its claim to such an extreme that it ends by actually weakening the mind of the mentally inferior or the child, so also the Eternal can in the imagination of an excitable person make an attempt to push the temporal into madness. But the grieving of repentance after God and the heartfelt anxiety must not, above all, be confused with impatience. Experience teaches that the right moment to repent is not always the one that is immediately present. For repentance in this precipitate moment when labored thoughts and various passions are acutely active or at least are strained by this unburdening may so easily be mistaken about that which is really to be repented. It can so easily be confused with its opposite, with the momentary feeling of contrition, that is, with impatience. It can so easily be confused with a painful agonizing sorrow after the world, that is, with impatience; with a desperate feeling of grief in itself, that is, with impatience. But impatience, no matter how long it continues to rage, never becomes repentance. However clouded, then, the mind becomes, the sobs of impatience no matter how violent they are, never become sobs of repentance. The tears of impatience lack the blessed fruitfulness. They are like empty clouds that bear no water, or like convulsive puffs of wind. On the other hand, if a man assumed an even heavier guilt, but at the same time improved and year after year went steadily forward in the good, it is certain that from year to year, as he advanced in the good, he would with greater intensity repent of his guilt, the guilt which year by year in a temporal sense he would be leaving further and further behind. For it is indeed the case that guilt must be alive for a man if he is honestly to repent. But just for that reason, precipitate repentance is false and is never to be sought after. For it may not be the inner anxiety of heart but only the momentary feeling that presents the guilt so actively. This kind of repentance is selfish, a matter of the senses, sensually powerful for the moment, excited in expression, impatient in the most diverse exaggerations—and, just on this account, is not real repentance. Sudden repentance would drink down all the bitterness of sorrow in a single draught and then hurry on. It wants to get away from guilt. It wants to banish all recollection of it, fortifying itself by imagining that it does this in order not to be held back in the pursuit of the Good. It is its wish that guilt, after a time, might be wholly forgotten. And once again, this is impatience. Perhaps a later sudden repentance may make it apparent that the former sudden repentance lacked true inwardness.

It is told that there was once a man who through his

misdeeds deserved the punishment which the law meted out to him. After he had suffered for his wrong acts he went back into ordinary society, improved. Then he went to a strange land, where he was not known, and where he became known for his worthy conduct. All was forgotten. Then one day there appeared a fugitive that recognized the distinguished person as his equal back in those miserable days. This was a terrifying memory to meet. A deathlike fear shook him each time this man passed. Although silent, this memory shouted in a high voice until through the voice of this vile fugitive it took on words. Then suddenly despair seized this man, who seemed to have been saved. And it seized him just because repentance was forgotten, because the improvement toward society was not the resigning of himself to God, so that in the humility of repentance he might remember what he had been. For in the temporal, and sensual, and social sense, repentance is in fact something that comes and goes during the years. But in the eternal sense, it is a silent daily anxiety. It is eternally false, that guilt is changed by the passage of a century. To assert anything of this sort is to confuse the Eternal with what the Eternal is least like— with human forgetfulness.

If anyone in a brazen and impious mood should pronounce absolution from the Good, on the ground that all is lost, then this is sacrilege and this will only add to the guilt by piling up more and more fresh guilt. Now let us indeed consider this. Guilt is not increased for the reason that it seems more and more tragic to the improved individual. It is not a gain that guilt should be wholly forgotten. On the contrary, it is loss and perdition. But it is a gain to win an inner intensity of heart through a deeper and deeper inner sorrowing over guilt. It is not a gain to notice, because of a man's forgetfulness, that he is growing older. But it is a gain to notice that a man has grown older by the deeper and deeper penetration into his heart of the transformation wrought by remorse. One should be able to tell the age of a tree from its bark; in truth one can also tell a man's age in the Good by the intensity of his repentance. There is a battle of despair that struggles—with the consequences. The enemy attacks constantly from behind, and yet the fighter shall continue to advance. When this is so, the repentance is still young and weak. There is a suffering of repentance, that is not impatient in bearing the punishment, but yet each moment cringes under it. When this is so, the repentance is still young and weak. There is a silent, sleepless sorrow at the picturing of what has been wasted. It does not despair, but in its daily grieving, it is always restless. When this is so, the repentance is still young and weak. There is a laborious moving forward in the Good that is like the gait of one whose feet are without skin. He is willing enough, he will gladly walk swiftly, but he has suffered a loss of courage. The pains make his going uncertain and agonizing. When this is so, the repentance is still young and weak.

But when, in spite of this, more confident steps are made along the way, when punishment itself becomes a blessing, when consequences even become redemptive, when progress in the Good is apparent; then is there a milder but deep sorrow that remembers the guilt. It has wearied out and overcome what could deceive and confuse the sight. Therefore it does not see falsely, but sees only the one sorrowful thing. This is the older, the strong and the powerful repentance. When it is a matter of the senses, it is true that they deteriorate and decline in the course of the years. Of a dancer one must say that her time is past when her youth is gone. But it is otherwise with a penitent. And it must be said of repentance that, if it is forgotten, then its strength was only an immaturity; but the longer and the more deeply one treasures it, the better it becomes. For guilt looks most terrifying the nearer at hand one sees it. But repentance is most acceptable to God, the further away repentance views the guilt, along the way of the Good.

So, then, repentance should not merely have its time, but even its time of preparation. Although it should be a silent daily concern, it should also be able to collect itself and be well prepared for the solemn occasion. One such an occasion is the office of Confession, the holy act for which preparation should be made in advance. As a man changes his raiment for a feast, so is a man changed in his heart who prepares himself for the holy act of confession. It is indeed like a changing of raiment to lay off manyness, in order rightly to center down upon one thing; to interrupt the busy course of activity, in order to put on the quiet of contemplation and be at one with oneself. And this being at one with oneself is the simple festival garment of the feast that is the condition of admittance. The manyness, one may see with a dispersed mind, see something of it, see it in passing, see it with half-closed eyes, with a divided mind, see it and indeed not see it. In the rush of busyness, one may be anxious over many things, begin many things, do many things at once, and only half do them all. But one cannot confess without this at-oneness with oneself. He that is not truly at one with himself during the hour of the office of Confession is merely dispersed. If he remains silent, he is not collected; if he speaks, it is only in a chatty vein, not in confession.

But he that in truth becomes at one with himself, he is in the silence. And this is indeed like a changing of raiment: to strip oneself of all that is as full of noise as it is empty, in order to be hidden in the silence, to become

open. This silence is the simple festivity of the holy act
of confession. For at dancing and festive occasions worldly
judgment holds that the more musicians, the better. But
when we are thinking of divine things, the deeper the
stillness the better. When the wanderer comes away from
the much-traveled noisy highway into places of quiet, then
it seems to him (for stillness is impressive) as if he must
examine himself, as if he must speak out what lies hidden
in the depths of his soul. It seems to him, according to the
poets' explanation, as if something inexpressible thrusts
itself forward from his innermost being, the unspeakable,
for which indeed language has no vessel of expression. Even
the longing is not the unspeakable itself. It is only a hastening after it. But what silence means, what the surroundings
will say in this stillness, is just the unspeakable.

Now the surprise expressed by the trees, if it can be said
that the trees looked down in surprise upon the wanderer,
explains nothing. And the wood's echo makes very clear
indeed that it explains nothing. No, as an impregnable
fortress throws back the attack of the enemy, so the echo
throws back the voice, no matter how loudly the wanderer
shouts. And the clouds hang as they please, and dream
only of themselves. Whether seeming to be in restful rev-
ery, or enjoying voluptuous soft movements; whether in
their transparence running swiftly off, driven by the wind,
or gathering in a dark mass to battle with the wind, at
least they do not trouble themselves over the wanderer.

And the sea, like a wise man, is sufficient unto itself.
Whether it lies like a child and amuses itself with its soft
ripples as a child that plays with its mouth, or at noon
lies like a drowsy thinker in carefree enjoyment and allows
its gaze to wander over all, or in the night ponders deeply
over its own being; whether in order to see what is going
on, it cunningly conceals itself as though it no longer

existed, or whether it rages in its own passion: the sea has a deep ground, it knows well enough what it knows. That which has that deep ground always knows this; but there is no sharing of this knowledge.

And what a puzzling arrangement the army of stars presents! Yet there seems to be an agreement between them that they shall arrange themselves in this fashion. But the stars are so far away that they cannot see the wanderer. It is only the wanderer who can see the stars, hence there may come no agreement between him and the stars. So this melancholy of poetical longing is grounded in a deep misunderstanding, because the lonely wanderer is everywhere surrounded in nature by that which does not understand him, even though it always seems as if an understanding must be arrived at.

Now the unspeakable is like the murmuring of a brook. If you go buried in your own thoughts, if you are busy, then you do not notice it at all in passing. You are not aware that this murmuring exists. But if you stand still, then you discover it. And if you have discovered it, then you must stand still. And when you stand still, then it persuades you. And when it has persuaded you, then you must stoop and listen attentively to it. And when you have stooped to listen to it, then it captures you. And when it has captured you, then you cannot break away from it, then you are overpowered. Infatuated, you sink down at its side. At each moment it is as if in the next moment it must offer an explanation. But the brook goes on murmuring, and the wanderer at its side grows older.

It is otherwise with one who confesses. The stillness also impresses him, yet not in the melancholy mood of misunderstanding, but rather with the seriousness of eternity. He is not, like the wanderer, uncertain about how he came upon the still places. Nor is he like the poet who wishes

to seek out loneliness and its mood. No, to confess is a
holy act, for which purpose, the mind is collected in preparation. That which environs you knows well enough what
this stillness means and that it calls for earnestness. It
knows that it is its wish to be understood. It knows that
fresh guilt is incurred if it be misunderstood. And the
One that is present at this confession is an omniscient One.
He knows and remembers all that this man has ever confided to Him, or that this man has ever withdrawn from
His confidence. He is an omniscient One that again at the
final moment of this man's life will remember this hour,
will remember what this man confided to Him and what
this man withdrew from His confidence. He is an omniscient One who knows every thought from a distance,
who knows plainly the very path of each thought, even
when it eludes a man's own consciousness. He is an
omniscient One "who seeth in secret," with whom a man
speaks even in silence, so that no one shall venture to
deceive Him either by talk, or by silence, as in this world
where one man can conceal much from the other now
by being silent, and again even more by talking.

The person making the confession is not like a servant
that gives account to his lord for the management which
is given over to him because the lord could not manage
all or be present in all places. The all-knowing One was
present at each instant for which reckoning shall be made
in the account. The account of what is done is not made
for the lord's sake but for the servant's sake, who must
even render account of how he used the very moment of
rendering the account. Nor is the person confessing like
one that confides in a friend to whom sooner or later he
reveals things that the friend did not previously know.
The all-knowing One does not get to know something
about the maker of the confession, rather the maker of

confession gets to know about himself. Therefore, do not raise the objection against the confession that there is no point in confiding to the all-knowing One that which He already knows. Reply first to the question whether it is not conferring a benefit when a man gets to know something about himself which he did not know before. A hasty explanation could assert that to pray is a useless act, because a man's prayer does not alter the unalterable. But would this be desirable in the long run? Could not fickle man easily come to regret that he had gotten God changed? The true explanation is therefore at the same time the one most to be desired. The prayer does not change God, but it changes the one who offers it. It is the same with the substance of what is spoken. Not God, but you, the maker of the confession, get to know something by your act of confession.

Much that you are able to keep hidden in darkness, you first get to know by your opening it to the knowledge of the all-knowing One. Even the most atrocious misdeeds are committed, even blood is spilt, and many times it must in truth be said of the guilty one: he knew not what he did. Perhaps he died, without ever in repentance really getting to know what it was he had done. For does passion ever properly know what it does? Does not passion's insidious temptation and its apparent excuse center in that deceptive ignorance about itself because, in the instant, it has forgotten the Eternal? For if passion continues in a man, it changes his life into nothing but instants and as passion cunningly serves its deluded master, it gradually gains the ascendancy until the master serves it like a blind serf!

For when hate, and anger, and revenge, and despondency, and melancholy, and despair, and fear of the future, and reliance on the world, and trust in oneself, and pride that infuses itself even into sympathy, and envy that even mingles itself with friendship, and that inclination that may have changed but not for the better: when these dwell in a man—when was it without the deceptive excuse of ignorance? And when a man remained ignorant of them, was it not precisely because he at the same time remained ignorant of the fact that there is an all-knowing One.

Yes, there is an ignorance which no one needs be troubled over if he was deprived either of the opportunity or the capacity to learn. But there is an ignorance about one's own life that is equally tragic for the learned and for the simple, for both are bound by the same responsibility. This ignorance is called self-deceit. There is an ignorance that by degrees, as more and more is learned, gradually changes into knowledge. But there is only one thing that can remove that other ignorance which is self-deception. And to be ignorant of the fact that there is one thing and only one thing, and that only one thing is necessary, is still to be in self-deception.

The ignorant one may have been ignorant of much. He can increase his knowledge, and still there is much that he does not know. But if the self-deluded one speaks of quantity, and of variety, then he is still in self-deception, still deeply ensnared by and in the grip of multiplicity. The ignorant man can gradually acquire wisdom and knowledge, but the self-deluded one if he won "the one thing needful" would have won purity of heart.

3. Barriers to Willing One Thing:

Variety and Great Moments Are Not One Thing

So LET us, then, upon the occasion of a time of Confession speak about this sentence: PURITY OF HEART IS TO WILL ONE THING as we base our meditation on the Apostle James' words in his Epistle, Chapter 4, verse 8:

"Draw nigh to God and he will draw nigh to you. Cleanse your hands, ye sinners; and purify your hearts ye double-minded." For only the pure in heart can see God, and therefore, draw nigh to Him; and only by God's drawing nigh to them can they maintain this purity. And he who in truth wills only one thing can will only the Good, and he who only wills one thing when he wills the Good can only will the Good in truth.

. . . . .

Let us speak of this, but let us first put out of our minds the occasion of the office of Confession in order to come to an agreement on an understanding of this verse, and on what the apostolic word of admonition "purify your hearts ye double-minded" is condemning, namely, *double-mindedness*. Then at the close of the talk we may return more specifically to a treatment of the occasion.

. . . . .

I. IF IT IS TO BE POSSIBLE, THAT A MAN CAN WILL ONLY ONE THING, THEN HE MUST WILL THE GOOD.

To will only one thing: but will this not inevitably become a long-drawn-out talk? If one should consider this

matter properly must he not first consider, one by one, each
goal in life that a man could conceivably set up for himself, mentioning separately all of the many things that a
man might will? And not only this; since each of these
considerations readily becomes too abstract in character,
is he not obliged as the next step to attempt to will, one
after the other, each of these goals in order to find out
what is the single thing he is to will, if it is a matter of
willing only one thing? Yes, if someone should begin in this
fashion, then he would never come to an end. Or more
accurately, how could he ever arrive at the end since at
the outset he took the wrong way and then continued to
go on further and further along this false way? It is only
by a painful route that this way leads to the Good, namely,
when the wanderer turns around and goes back. For as
the Good is only a single thing, so all ways lead to the
Good, even the false ones: when the repentant one follows
the same way back. Oh, Thou the unfathomable trustworthiness of the Good! Wherever a man may be in the
world, whichever road he travels, when he wills one thing,
he is on a road that leads him to Thee! Here such a far-
flung enumeration would only work harm. Instead of
wasting many moments on naming the vast multitude of
goals or squandering life's costly years in personal experi-
ments upon them, can the talk do as life ought to do—with
a commendable brevity stick to the point?

In a certain sense nothing can be spoken of so briefly as
the Good, when it is well described. For the Good without
condition and without qualification, without preface and
without compromise is, absolutely the only thing that a
man may and should will, and is only one thing. Oh,
blessed brevity, oh, blessed simplicity, that seizes swiftly
what cleverness, tired out in the service of vanity, may

grasp but slowly! That which a simple soul, in the happy
impulse of a pious heart, feels no need of understanding
in an elaborate way, since he simply seizes the Good immediately, is grasped by the clever one only at the cost
of much time and much grief. The way this one thing is
willed is not such that: one man wills one thing but that
which he wills is not the Good; another wills one thing
nor is what he wills the Good; a third wills one thing
and what he wills *is* the Good. No, it is not done in that
way. The person who wills one thing that is not the Good,
he does not truly will one thing. It is a delusion, an illusion, a deception, a self-deception that he wills only one
thing. For in his innermost being he is, he is bound to be,
double-minded. Therefore the Apostle says, "Purify your
hearts ye double-minded," that is, purify your hearts of
double-mindedness; in other words, let your heart in truth
will only one thing, for therein is the heart's purity.

And again it is of this same purity of heart that the
Apostle is speaking when he says, "If someone lacks wisdom, then let him pray . . . but in faith, not like a
double-minded man" (James I:5, 6, 8). For purity of heart
is the very wisdom that is acquired through prayer. A
man of prayer does not pore over learned books for he is
the wise man "whose eyes are opened"—when he kneels
down (Numbers 24:16).

In a word, then, there is a man whose mind remains
piously ignorant of the multitude of things, for the Good
is one thing. The more difficult part of the talk is directed
to the man whose mind in its double-mindedness has made
the doubtful acquaintance of the multitude of things, and
of knowledge. If it is certain that a man in truth wills
one thing, then he wills the Good, for this alone can be
willed in this manner. But both of these assertions speak
of identical things, or they speak of different things. The

one assertion plainly designates the name of the Good, declaring it to be that one thing. The other assertion cunningly conceals this name. It appears almost as if it spoke of something else. But just on that account it forces its way, searchingly, into a man's innermost being. And no matter how much he may protest, or defy, or boast that he wills only one thing, it searches him through and through in order to show the double-mindedness in him if the one thing he wills is not the Good.

For in truth there was a man on earth who seemed to will only one thing. It was unnecessary for him to insist upon it. Even if he had been silent about it, there were witnesses enough against him who testified how inhumanly he steeled his mind, how nothing touched him, neither tenderness, nor innocence, nor misery; how his blinded soul had eyes for nothing, and how the senses in him had only eyes for the one thing that he willed. And yet it was certainly a delusion, a terrible delusion, that he willed one thing. For pleasure and honor and riches and power and all that this world has to offer only appear to be one thing. It is not, nor does it remain one thing, while everything else is in change or while he himself is in change. It is not in all circumstances the same. On the contrary, it is subject to continual alteration. Hence even if this man named but one thing whether it be pleasure, or honor or riches, actually he did not will one thing. Neither can he be said to will one thing when that one thing which he wills is not in itself one: is in itself a multitude of things, a dispersion, the toy of changeableness, and the prey of corruption! In the time of pleasure see how he longed for one gratification after another. Variety was his watchword. Is variety, then, to will one thing that shall ever remain the same? On the contrary, it is to will one thing that must never be the same. It is to will a multitude of things. And a person who wills in this fashion is not only double-minded but is at odds with himself. For such a man wills first one thing and then immediately wills the opposite, because the oneness of pleasure is a snare and a delusion. It is the diversity of pleasures that he wills. So when the man of whom we are speaking had gratified himself up to the point of disgust, he became weary and sated. Even if he still desired one thing—what was it that he desired? He desired new pleasures; his enfeebled soul raged so that no ingenuity was sufficient to discover something new— something new! It was change he cried out for as pleasure served him, change! change! And it was change that he cried out for as he came to pleasure's limit, as his servants were worn out—change! change!

Now it is to be understood that there are also changes in life that can prove to a man whether he wills one thing. There is the change of the perishable nature when the sensual man must step aside, when dancing and the tumult of the whirling senses are over, when all becomes soberly quiet. That is the change of death. If, for once, the perisha-ble nature should seem to forget to close in, if it should seem as if the sensual one had succeeded in slipping by: death does not forget. The sensual one will not slip past death, who has dominion over what belongs to the earth and who will change into nothing the one thing which the sensual person desires.

And last of all, there is the change of eternity, which changes all. Then only the Good remains and it remains the blessed possession of the man that has willed only one thing. But that rich man whom no misery could touch, that rich man who even in eternity to his own damnation must continue to will one thing, ask him now whether he really wills one thing. So, too, with honor and riches and power. For in the time of strength as he aspired to honor, did he really discover some limit, or was that not simply the striver's restless passion to climb higher and higher? Did he find some rest amid his sleeplessness in which he sought to capture honor and to hold it fast? Did he find some refreshment in the cold fire of his passion? And if he really won honor's highest prize, then is earthly honor in itself one thing? Or in its diversity when the thousands and thousands braid the wreath, is honor to be likened to the gorgeous carpet of the field—created by a single hand? No, like worldly contempt, worldly honor is a whirlpool, a play of confused forces, an illusory moment in the flux of opinions. It is a sense-deception, as when a swarm of insects at a distance seem to the eye like one body; a sense-deception, as when the noise of the many at a distance seems to the ear like a single voice.

Even if honor were unanimous it would still be meaningless, and the more so, the more thousands that create the unanimity. And the greater the multitude that created unanimity, the sooner will it show itself to be meaningless. And indeed it was this unanimity of the thousands that he desired. It was not the approbation of the good men. They are soon counted. No, it was rather the approbation of the thousands. Is, then, this desire for counting, is this to will one thing? To count and count until it suffices, to count and count until a mistake is made; is this to will one thing? Whoever, therefore, wills this honor or fears this contempt, whether or not he is said to will one thing in his innermost being, is not merely double-minded but thousand-minded, and at variance with himself. So is his life when he must grovel—in order to attain honor; when he must flatter his enemies—in order to attain honor; when he must woo the favor of those he despises—in order to attain honor; when he must betray the one whom he respects—in order to attain honor. For to attain honor means to despise oneself after one has attained the pinnacle of honor—and yet to tremble before any change. Change, yes, where does change rage more unchecked than here? What desertion is more swift and sudden, like a mistake in foolery, like a hit by a blind man, when the seeker for honor has not even time to take off the garb of honor before insult seizes him in it? Change, the final change, the absolute certainty among the range of unpredictables: no matter how loud the thunder of honor may sound over his grave, even if it could be heard over the whole earth, there is one who cannot hear it: the dead man, he who died with honor, the single thing he had desired. But also in dying he lost the honor, for it remains outside, it marches home again, it dies away like an echo. Change, the true change, when eternity exists: I should like to know if honor's crown is offered to the much-honored one there! And yet eternity is more just than the earth and the world; for in eternity there is a crown of honor laid aside for each of those that have in truth willed only one thing. So also with riches and power and the world that passes away and the lust thereof. The one who has willed either of them, even if he only willed one thing, must, to his own agony, continue to will it when it has passed, and learn by the agony of contradiction that it is not one thing. But the one who in truth willed one thing and therefore willed the Good, even if he be sacrificed for it, why should he not go on willing the same in eternity, the same thing that he was willing to die for? Why should he not will the same, when it has triumphed in eternity?

To will one thing, therefore, cannot mean to will that which only appears to be one thing. The fact is that the worldly goal is not one thing in its essence because it is unreal. Its so-called unity is actually nothing but emptiness which is hidden beneath the manyness. In the short-lived moment of delusion the worldly goal is therefore a multitude of things, and thus not one thing. So far is it from a state of being and remaining one thing, that in the next moment it changes itself into its opposite. Carried to its extreme limit, what is pleasure other than disgust? What is earthly honor at its dizzy pinnacle other than contempt for existence? What are riches, the highest superabundance of riches, other than poverty? For no matter how much all the earth's gold hidden in covetousness may amount to, is it not infinitely less than the smallest mite hidden in the contentment of the poor! What is worldly omnipotence other than dependence? What slave in chains is as unfree as a tyrant! No, the worldly goal is not one thing. Diverse as it is, in life it is changed into its opposite, in death into nothing, in eternity into damnation: for the one who has willed this goal. Only the Good is one thing in its essence and the same in each of its expressions. Take love as an illustration. The one who truly loves does not love once and for all. Nor does he use a part of his love, and then again another part. For to change it into small coins is not to use it rightly. No, he loves with all of his love. It is wholly present in each expression. He continues to give it away as a whole, and yet he keeps it intact as a whole, in his heart. Wonderful riches! When the miser has gathered all the world's gold in sordidness—then he has become poor. When the lover gives away his whole love, he keeps it entire—in the purity of the heart. Shall a man in truth will one thing, then this one thing that he wills must be such that it remains unaltered in all changes, so that by willing it he can win immutability. If it changes continually, then he himself becomes changeable, double-minded, and unstable. And this continual change is nothing else than impurity.

Now, willing one thing does not mean to commit the grave mistake of a brazen, unholy enthusiasm, namely, to will the big, no matter whether it be good or bad. Also, one who wills in this fashion no matter how desperately he does it, is indeed double-minded. Is not despair simply double-mindedness? For what is despairing other than to have two wills? For whether the weakling despairs over not being able to wrench himself away from the bad, or whether the brazen one despairs over not being able to tear himself completely away from the Good: they are both double-minded, they both have two wills. Neither of them honestly wills one thing, however desperately they may seem to will it. Whether it was a woman whom desire brought to desperation, or whether it was a man who despaired in defiance; whether a man despaired because he got his will, or despaired because he did not get his will: each one in despairing has two wills, one that he fruitlessly tries wholly to follow and one that he fruitlessly tries wholly to avoid. In this fashion has God, better than any king, insured himself against every rebellion. For it has indeed happened that a king has been dethroned by a rebellion. But each rebel against God, in the last instance, is himself reduced to despair. Despair is the limit—"here and no further!" Despair is the limit. Here are met the cowardly timorous ill-temper of self-love, and the proud defiant presumption of the mind—here they are met in equal impotence.

Only too soon personal experience and the experience of others teaches how far most men's lives are from being what a man's life ought to be. All have great moments. They see themselves in the magic mirror of possibility which hope holds before them while the wish flatters them. But they swiftly forget this sight in the daily round of things. Or perhaps they talk enthusiastic words, "for the

tongue is a little member and boasteth great things."[5] But
talk takes the name of enthusiasm in vain by proclaiming
loudly from the housetop what it should work out in
silence. And in the midst of the trivial details of life these
enthusiastic words are quickly forgotten. It is forgotten
that such a thing was said of this man. It is forgotten that
it was he himself who said it. Now and then, perhaps,
memory wakens with horror, and remorse seems to promise
new strength. But, alas, this, too, lasts only for a good-
sized moment. All of them have intentions, plans, resolutions for life, yes, for eternity. But the intention soon
loses its youthful strength and fades away. The resolution
is not firmly grounded and is unable to withstand opposition. It totters before circumstances and is altered by them.
Memory, too, has a way of failing, until by common practice and habit they learn to draw sympathy from one
another. If someone proclaims the slender comfort that
excuses yield, instead of realizing how treacherous is such
sympathy, they finally come to regard it as edifying,
because it encourages and strengthens indolence. Now there
are men who find it edifying that the demand to will one
thing be asserted in all its sublimity, in all its severity, so
that it may press its claim into the innermost fastness of
the soul. Others find it edifying, that a wretched compromise should be made between God, the claim, and the
language used. There are men who find it edifying if only
someone will challenge them. But there are also the sleepy
souls who regard it as not only pleasing, but even edifying,
to be lulled to sleep.

This is indeed a lamentable fact; but there is a wisdom
which is not from above, but is earthly and fleshly and
devilish. It has discovered this common human weakness
and indolence; it wants to be helpful. It perceives that all
depends upon the will and so it proclaims loudly, "Unless

it wills one thing, a man's life is sure to become one of
wretched mediocrity, of pitiful misery. He must will one
thing regardless of whether it be good or bad. He must
will one thing for therein lies a man's greatness." Yet it is
not difficult to see through this powerful error. As to the
working out of salvation, the holy Scripture teaches that
sin is the corruption of man. Salvation, therefore, lies only
in the purity with which a man wills the Good. That very
earthly and devilish cleverness distorts this into a temptation to perdition; weakness is a man's misfortune; strength
the sole salvation: "When the unclean spirit is gone out of
a man, he walketh through dry and empty places but finds
no rest. Then he turns back again and now he brings with
him" that unclean cleverness, the wisdom of the desert
and the empty places, that unclean cleverness—that now
drives out the spirit of indolence and of mediocrity "so
that the last stage becomes worse than the first."[6] How
shall one describe the nature of such a man? It is said of a
singer that by overscreeching he can crack his voice. In like
fashion, such a man's nature by overscreeching itself and
the voice of conscience, has cracked. It is said of a man
who stands dizzily upon a high place, that all things run
together before his eyes. Such a man has made himself
giddy in the infinite, where those things which are forever
separate run together into one thing, so that only the vast
remains.

It is this dryness and emptiness that always gives birth
to giddiness. But no matter how desperately such a man
may seem to will one thing, he is double-minded. If he,
the self-willed one, had his way, then there would be only
this one thing: he would be the only one that was not
double-minded, he the only one that had cast off every
chain, he the only one that was free. But the slave of sin
is not yet free; nor has he cast off the chain, "because he

scoffs at it."[7] He is in bonds, and therefore double-minded, and for once he may not have his own way. There is a power that binds him. He cannot tear himself loose from it. Nay, he cannot even wholly will it. For this power, too, is denied him. If you, my listener, should see such a man, although it is unlikely, for without a doubt weakness and mediocrity are the more common, if you should meet him in what he himself would call a weak moment, but which, alas, you would have to call a better moment; if you should meet him when he had found no rest in the desert, when the giddiness passes away for a moment and he feels an agonizing longing for the Good; if you should meet him when, shaken in his innermost being, and not without sadness, he was thinking of that man of single purpose who even in all his frailty still wills the Good: then you would discover that he had two wills, and you would discover his painful double-mindedness.

Desperate as he was, he thought: lost is lost. But he could not help turning around once more in his longing for the Good. How terribly embittered he had become against this very longing, a longing that reveals that, just as a man in all his defiance has not power enough wholly to loose himself from the Good, because it is the stronger, so he has not even the power wholly to will it.

Perhaps you may even have heard that desperate one say, "Some good went down with me." When a man meets his death by drowning, as he sinks, without being quite dead he comes to the surface again. At last a bubble comes out of his mouth. When this has happened, then he sinks, dead. That bubble was the last breath, the last supply of air, that could make him lighter than the sea. So with that remark. In that remark the last hope of salvation expired. In that remark he gave himself up. Was there still concealed in this thought a hope of salvation? Hidden in the soul, was there still in this thought a possible link with salvation? When a remark is pronounced in confidence to another man (oh, terrible misuse of confidence, even if the desperate one only misused it against himself!), when this word is heard, then he sinks forever.

Alas, it is horrible to see a man rush toward his own destruction. It is horrible to see him dance on the rim of the abyss without any intimation of it. But this clarity about himself and about his own destruction is even more horrible. It is horrible to see a man seek comfort by hurling himself into the whirlpool of despair. But this coolness is still more horrible: that, in the anxiety of death, a man should not cry out for help, "I am going under, save me"; but that he should quietly choose to be a witness to his own destruction! Oh, most extreme vanity, not to wish to draw man's eyes to himself by beauty, by riches, by ability, by power, by honor, but to wish to get his attention by his own destruction, by choosing to say of himself what at most pity in all sadness may venture to say of such a person at his grave, "Yet, some good went down with him." Oh, horrible doubleness of mind in a man's destruction, to wish to draw a sort of advantage out of the fact that the Good remains the only thing that a man has not willed. For now the other will becomes apparent to him, even if it were so weak as to be but a feeble dallying in the moment of destruction, an attempt to be exceptional by means of his own destruction.

To will one thing cannot, then, mean to will what in its essence is not one thing, but only seems to be so by means of a horrible falsehood. Only through a lie is it one thing. Now just as he that only wills this one thing is a liar, so he that conjures up this one thing is the father of lies. That dryness and emptiness is not in truth one thing, but is in truth nothing at all. And it is destruction for the man that only wills that one. If, on the contrary, a man should in truth will only one thing, then this thing must, in the truth of its innermost being, be one thing. It must, by an eternal separation, cut off the heterogeneous from itself in order that it may in truth continue to be one and the same thing and thereby fashion that man who only wills one thing into conformity with itself.

In truth to will one thing, then, can only mean to will the Good, because every other object is not a unity; and the will that only wills that object, therefore, must become double-minded. For as the coveted object is, so becomes the coveter. Or would it be possible that a man by willing the evil could will one thing, provided that it was possible for a man so to harden himself as to will nothing but the evil? Is not this evil, like evil persons, in disagreement with itself, divided against itself? Take one such man, separate him from society, shut him up in solitary confinement. Is he not at odds with himself there, just as a poor union between persons of his sort is an association that is ridden with dissension? But a good man, even if he lived in an out-of-the-way corner of the world and never saw any human being, would be at one with himself and at one with all about him because he wills one thing, and because the Good is one thing. *Each one who in truth would will one thing must be led to will the Good*, even though now and then it happens that a man begins by willing one thing that is not in its deepest sense the Good although it may be something quite innocent; and then, little by little, he is changed really in truth to will one thing by willing the Good. Love, from time to time, has in this way helped a man along the right path. Faithfully he only willed one thing, his love. For it, he would live and die. For it, he would sacrifice all and in it alone he would have his eternal reward. Yet the act of being

in love is still not in the deepest sense the Good. But it
may possibly become for him a helpful educator, who will
finally lead him by the possession of his beloved one or
perhaps by her loss, in truth to will one thing and to will
the Good. In this fashion a man is educated by many
means; and true love is also an education toward the Good.

Perhaps there was a man whose enthusiasm reached out
toward a definite cause. In his enthusiasm he desired
only one thing. He would live and die for that cause.
He would sacrifice all for that in which alone he would
have his happiness, for love and enthusiasm are not satisfied
with a divided heart. Yet his endeavor was perhaps still not
in the deepest sense the Good. Thus enthusiasm became for
him a teacher, whom he outgrew, but to whom also he
owed much. For, as it is said, all ways lead to the Good,
when a man in truth only wills one thing. And where
there is some truth in the fact that he wills one thing, this
is all for the best. But there is danger that the lover and
the enthusiast may swerve out of the true course and aim
perhaps for the impressive instead of being led to the Good.
The Good is certainly also in truth the impressive, but the
impressive is not always the Good. And one can bid for a
woman's favor by willing something when it is merely
impressive. This can flatter the girl's pride and she can
repay it with her adoration. But God in heaven is not as
a young girl's folly. He does not reward the impressive
with admiration. The reward of the good man is to be
allowed to worship in truth.

4. Barriers to Willing One Thing:
The Reward-Disease

II. IF IT BE POSSIBLE FOR A MAN REALLY IN
TRUTH TO WILL ONE THING, THEN HE MUST
WILL THE GOOD IN TRUTH.

A. IF IT BE POSSIBLE FOR A MAN TO WILL THE GOOD IN
TRUTH, THEN HE MUST BE AT ONE WITH HIMSELF IN
WILLING TO RENOUNCE ALL DOUBLE-MINDEDNESS.

*Therefore, if it be possible for a man to will one thing,
then he must will the Good, for only the Good is one.
Thus if it becomes a fact that he wills one thing, he
must will the Good in truth.*

OH, THAT one might be able, at this point, to
speak rightly! For at this point what the talk is concerned
with is the life that most men lead: they desire the Good,
and yet the world is still so filled with double-mindedness.
Here, too, the speaker has his own life, his own frailties, his
own share of doubleness of mind. Oh, that the talk might
not seem to wish to judge or accuse others. For to wish to
judge others instead of one's self would also be double-
mindedness. Oh, that the talk might not seem to press
demands that are binding upon others but that exempt the
speaker, as if he had only the task of talking. For this,
too, is double-mindedness, just as it is hidden pride to wish
to offer comfort to others but not to be willing to let
oneself be comforted. No matter how adroitly, by means
of a sad or cheerful mood, he knows how in sympathy
to console others, if at the same time he believes that for

himself there is no consolation, this is hidden pride and
so double-mindedness. Oh, that one might wound no one
except to his healing; that the talk might embitter no
one and yet be the truth, that the talk along with truth
might be sufficiently penetrating to reveal that which is
hidden! Oh, that the talk might wipe out double-mindedness and win hearts for the Good! Yet not by persuasion.
For this also readily becomes double-minded, to wish to
enjoy the pleasure of persuading, to treasure the longing
for it, to quiet oneself by it—and thereby forget what is
to be done. Oh, that the talk might repel the listeners from
the speaker and attract them only to the Good!

1. *In the first place a statement must be made which is easy
to grasp: that the man who desires the Good for the sake
of the reward does not will one thing, but is double-
minded.*

The Good is one thing; the reward is another that may
be present and may be absent for the time being, or until
the very last. When he, then, wills the Good for the sake
of the reward, he does not will one thing but two. It is
now certain that he will not in this way make much
progress along the pathway of the Good. For in truth it is
as if a man, instead of naturally using both eyes to see
one thing, should use one eye to see one side and the other
eye to see the other side. This does not succeed. It only confuses sight. However, we are not speaking about this here,
except to note that it is double-mindedness. In ancient
times this problem was also frequently an object of consideration. There were shameless teachers of impudence[8]
who thought it right to do wrong on a large scale and then
to make it appear as if one willed the Good. In this way
they thought one had a double advantage: the pitiful
advantage of being able to do wrong, to be able to get one's
own way, to let one's passions rage, and the hypocritical

advantage of seeming to be good. But in ancient times there was also a simple sage, whose simplicity became a snare for the impudent ones' sophistry. He taught that in order really to be certain that it was the Good that man willed, one ought even to shun seeming good, presumably in order that the reward should not become tempting. For so different is the Good and the reward, when the reward is separately striven after, that the Good is the ennobling and the sanctifying; the reward is the tempting. But the tempting is never the Good. This reward, that we are talking about here, is the world's reward. For the reward which God for eternity has joined with the Good has nothing bad in it. It is also quite certain. Neither things present nor things to come, nor height nor depth, can separate it from the Good.[9] Angels cannot will such separation and all the devils are not strong enough to accomplish it. But if the world itself is not Good in its innermost being; if, as the Scripture says, it still "lieth in wickedness,"[10] or if it is far from being as one for whom it is a rare exception not to will the Good; if this be so, then earthly reward is of a doubtful character. And hence it is all the more likely that the world will reward what it takes for the Good, what to a certain degree resembles the Good, what, as those impudent ones taught, has the Good's appearance—and those impudent ones were not lacking in intimate knowledge of the world. Hence reward is indeed that which tempts.

The question is not difficult. If a man loves a girl for the sake of her money, who will call him a lover? He does not love the girl, but the money. He is not a lover but a money-seeker. But if a man said, "It is the girl I love and she has money," and he should ask us for our judgment, for we have no particular call to judge, then a good answer would be, "It is a difficult matter with this money. Money may have a great influence, one can easily be deceived, and it is very difficult to know oneself." If he were really very intent on this matter he could even wish that the money were not there, just to test his love. For a true lover would say, "The girl has only one fault, she has money."

And what now may the girl say! If she said, "The advantage I wish to have is that it is I that have made him rich," I wonder if she could be called a real lover? For she did not really love him, but the money. If, on the contrary, the two in their love agreed to do a good act with this money which was a hindrance to them, then it would be made possible for them to desire love alone. Let us hope that no one would set about to disturb the innocent fancy of this beautiful thought by telling us, "What life will surely teach that pair!" Alas, there is a wretched knowledge, a shabby acquaintance with the real, that is not merely wretched and shabby but also on all occasions puts on an important front. As though that knowledge were anything but infamy in any person who in a cowardly and traitorous and envious and empty puffed-up manner dares to make such a comment! As if that knowledge were other than contemptible double-mindedness that both wills and does not will, and therefore will only lie, lie about the Good, and lie about the man who is good. Yes, what was once said of memory is applicable to that sort of knowledge, namely, that one might prefer to learn the art of forgetting.[11] Indeed it is easy enough for one to become schooled in that sort of knowledge. It may be learned readily enough from all the wretched ones, so that one might rather wish and pray, that there was an art that one could learn that would teach him to remain ignorant of such knowledge.

Now about desiring the girl without the money. Let us consider the Good, where all is on a more perfect plane, where earnestness and truth are the innocent fancy of

beautiful thought. To will the Good for the sake of reward is double-mindedness. To will one thing is, therefore,
to will the Good without considering the reward. In truth
to will one thing is to will the Good, but not, therefore,
to desire reward in the world. The reward can of course
come without a man's willing it. Even though it is in the
outward realms, the reward may come from God. But when
a man considers that all reward in the outer realm can
become what the world's reward always is—a temptation
for him, then he must guard himself even against true
reward just in order rightly to be able to will the Good.
Oh, that he might not forget, that this, even such a desire
to guard himself, may once more be a temptation to pride.

But if it be true of the reward for Good in the world,
that the reward the world gives is so dangerous, then the
Good has almost an edifying quality here in this world
(even if this edification is somewhat softened in the blessed
smile of eternity). For here the man who in truth wills the
Good, by willing one thing, is very rarely led into the difficulty of being tempted by reward. Now, that the Good
has its own reward is indeed forever certain. There is
nothing so certain. It is not even more certain that God
exists, for that is one and the same thing. But here on
earth, Good is often temporarily rewarded by ingratitude,
by lack of appreciation, by poverty, by contempt, by many
sufferings, and now and then by death. It is not this reward
to which we refer when we say that the Good has its
reward. Yet this is the reward that comes in the external
world and that comes first of all. And it is precisely this
reward which the man is anxious about, who wills the Good
for the sake of the reward. For he has no time to wait, no
time, no years, no life to give away—for an eternity.
Hence that reward which comes in the external world is
so far from being desirable, that, on the contrary, it is

both valuable and encouraging when it does not come in the outer world, so that the double-mindedness in the inner realm may perish, and so that the reward in heaven may be all the greater.

To will the Good for the sake of the reward is, as it were, a symbol of double-mindedness. And a double-minded man according to the Apostle James' words is, "unsteady in all his ways." Nor does he accomplish anything. For a double-minded man, says the same Apostle, may not expect to receive that for which he prays. Even if such a double-minded one, who wills the Good for the sake of the reward, may puff himself up, appear defiant, and fancy that he has won his goal, even if many blind ones foolishly think the same; yet let us not deceive each other, my listener, or allow a sense-deception to do so. It is quite possible that he will win good things, that are called reward. Still he does not get them as reward, at least not in truth, if it be true that to will the Good in truth is recognizable by one's willing it without reward. Oh, Thou the Good's wonderful at-oneness with thyself that protects thee from being deceived! When, for the sake of the reward, a double-minded person only pretends to will the Good, and he seems to get the reward, nevertheless he does not get it. For that which he gets, he does not get as reward—for the Good. So far is he from getting it as reward that rather at the very moment that he receives the Good, he discovers that the reward has vanished.

Look at the girl who has money. A false lover can perhaps deceive her, so that it appears as if he loved her, although what he really loves is the money. She may joyfully, perhaps even gratefully, continue to live in the fantasy that she is loved. But no one can deceive the Good, nay, not in all eternity! Not in all eternity! Yes, it is just there that one has the least chance of deceiving it. Per-

haps here on earth it can be accomplished; not that the
Good is deceived, but men may be deceived by the likeness
of the Good. Such does not escape the attention of the
Good. From time to time it focuses its wrath on such a
man and reveals his deception. But often the Good lets
the deceiver go his way because the Good knows, in itself,
that it is the stronger. Only a weak and effeminate man
demands immediate justification, demands immediate success in the outer world, just because he is weak, and therefore must have an outward proof—that he is the strongest.
The one who is really strong and is really the more powerful, quietly concedes a domain to the weakling and readily
allows him to give the impression of being the stronger.
So with the Good, when it tolerates such a deceiver, it is
as if it said to him secretly, "Yes, enjoy yourself with your
false appearance, but remember, we two, we shall talk
together again."

The double-minded one stands at a parting of the ways.
Two visions appear: the Good and the reward. It is not in
his power to bring them into agreement, for they are
fundamentally different from each other. Only that reward which God for all eternity adds to the Good in the
inner realm, only that is in truth homogeneous with the
Good. So he stands pondering and reflecting. If he is wholly
absorbed in his pondering, then he continues to stand—a
symbol of double-mindedness. But suppose he should tear
himself free from the deliberation and should now go forward. Along which way? Ah, do not ask him about that.
Perhaps he is able to answer learned questions and to betray extensive knowledge. But one thing he cannot do,
one and only one thing he is not able to do: he cannot
answer the question about which of the two ways he is
taking. By repeated thoughtful pondering in an attempt
to see the heterogeneous together, he has somewhat con-

fused his sight. He believes he has found that there is a
third way and that it is this third way along which he
is going. This third way has no name. For it does not
really exist, and so it is obvious that he, if he is sincere,
cannot say which way he is taking. If he is sincere, for
otherwise he would indeed declare that he is going along
the way of the Good, it may even be important to convince men of that—in order that they may honor him.
For honor belongs to the reward which he is seeking after.
The third way is the secret which he keeps to himself. And
now how does he go along this third way which is narrower than any rope-dancer's rope, for it simply does not
exist? Does he go steadily and firmly like one that has a
definite goal before his eyes; like one that scarcely looks
at anything around him in order not to be disturbed; like
one that looks for one thing alone—for the goal? No, only
a person upon the path of the Good walks in this fashion
with only the Good before his eyes.

Does he, then, go like the one that is hunting for every
sensation along the broad way of pleasure? No, that he
does not do. Does he go like a carefree youth who lightheartedly lets his gaze wander over everything about him
on his way? Alas, he is too old for that. How does he go,
then? He walks so slowly under the circumstances, because of the difficulty of the way. He feels his way forward
with his foot and as he finally plants his foot and takes a
step, he immediately looks about at the clouds, notes the
way the wind blows, and whether the smoke goes straight
up from the chimney. It is, namely, the reward—earth's
reward—that he is looking for. And that reward is like the
clouds and like the wind and like the smoke of the chimney. And so he asks his way continually. He gives minute
attention to the faces of the passing people in order to
learn how the reward stands, what the prices are, what

demands the time and the people would place upon the Good if they were to give the reward.

What is he really after? Nay, do not ask him about that. Perhaps he would be able to answer every other question with the exception of that one about the way. But this question he cannot answer in definite terms, if he is to answer it sincerely, for the reason that the answer is all too readily at hand: that he wills the Good and detests vice—when vice seems to be loathsome; that he wills the approbation of good people—when they are in the majority and possess the power; that he will benefit the good cause— when it is so good as to confer some advantage upon him. Yet in sincerity he dares not say definitely what he wills. He dares not say loudly and decisively with the full voice of conviction that he wills the Good. He utters it with the dull caution of double-mindedness. For he knows well enough that the Good and the reward are not rationed out together. Let us assume, that by such a careless utterance the Good and the reward came into conflict, and let us assume that he be considered as willing the Good in this manner. Now suppose that the reward is missing, which has previously happened in this world. What would he do then? Would he will the Good and even be willing to forego the appearance of willing the Good? No, definitely not. Does he, then, will the reward? Yes, but he will not plainly admit it. Does he, then, will the Good? Yes, now and then, perhaps, for decency's sake, as it is called. He pretends, therefore, to will the Good—for the sake of honor and reward. As a matter of fact he does occasionally will the Good—to save his face.

This is what happens to the man who hankers after a reward. He is so double-minded that one hardly knows whether to laugh or to weep over him, if one does not know that all double-mindedness is destruction. But if one knows this, he knows well enough what to do, especially when he has his own share of this double-mindedness.

Now this matter of willing the Good for the sake of reward may take a somewhat different form. Perhaps there was a man who really in all sincerity willed the Good. Humbly before God, and quickened in his enthusiasm, he cheerfully understood when the world and when men worked against him. He cheerfully understood that this opposition was the reward, and that there was nothing further to be said about it. Strengthened by God, bracing himself only by his confidence, he almost never desired to be rewarded in any other way by this world. But then he became weary. He clutched after the reward in the narrower sense, and after an easier understanding of the reward. For in general the closer the understanding lies to misunderstanding, the easier it becomes. He could not bear with the Eternal. He could not endure the opposition of the world and of the people. So first he claimed the reward, under the interpretation that there ought to be an agreement between the Good and the world. Finally, he demanded the reward alone. In this fashion he slipped backwards. Oh, sad end to a good beginning! Oh, Thou the Good's stern zeal for thyself, that Thou perhaps permittest him to get the reward in the world, just when Thou hast rejected him; that Thou lettest him get the reward of the world, while he has ungratefully forgotten what a blessedness it is to have Thy reward, while earth withholds her reward from him!

Or he did not begin so high, but simply with willing the Good in truth. Without knowledge of the world, without having conceived in his heart the possibility of what may happen to a man, he piously hoped that the Good would not withhold its reward. Now understood in the light of eternity, this is an eternal and sacred truth. But

in the sense of temporal existence, it is foolish and fruitless cleverness. So he went out into the school of experience,
for we all go to school as long as we live. Life's school is
for adults and therefore is somewhat more stern than the
children's school, where the attentive and industrious ones
come to the fore among those of the same age. So life took
him into its stern school. But he resisted. He reduced his
demands. He did not wish to deceive the Good. Alas,
neither would that help. He believed that as long as he
clung to the Good, he possessed a claim upon life. Now
it seemed to him as though the Good alone had claims
upon him. At this his courage slackened. He looked about
him where so many others helped themselves to the reward.
The tempter began to frighten him into a feeling of faint-
heartedness as to why he did not wish to be like the others
and as to why he insisted upon running after the vagaries
of imagination instead of laying hold of that which is
certain. Then his mind was changed. In life it happened to
him just as in school it might happen to the superior pupil
if there were no teacher. The mediocre would gain the
dominance and gain power to seduce the superior pupils,
because the good pupil had no teacher in whom to seek
protection. And in life there is no visible teacher who encourages the good pupil, for we are all pupils. If the good
pupil keeps on, he must find the encouragement in himself.
This he did not find. His courage was shattered. Perhaps
he did not find what he now sought in the world. And so
he went down, he the deceived one, whom the world deceived as to the reward, when he willed the Good and whom
the world betrayed most terribly, when it got him to forsake the Good.

5. Barriers to Willing One Thing:
Willing Out of Fear of Punishment

2. Next, it must be said that the man who only wills the
Good out of fear of punishment does not will one thing.
He is double-minded.

T HE OTHER aspect of the reward-centered man is
willing the good only out of fear of punishment. For in
essence, this is the same as to will the Good for the sake
of the reward, to the extent that avoiding an evil is an
advantage of the same sort as that of attaining a benefit.
The Good is one thing. Punishment is something else.
Therefore the double-minded person does not desire one
thing when he desires the Good under the condition that
he shall avoid punishment. The condition lays its finger
upon just the double-mindedness. If that condition were
not there, he would not fear the punishment, for punishment is indeed not what a man should fear. He should fear
to do wrong. But if he has done wrong, then he must, if
he really wills one thing and sincerely wills the Good, desire to be punished, that the punishment may heal him
just as medicine heals the sick. If one who is sick fears
the bitterness of the medicine, or fears "to let himself be
cut and cauterized by the physician," then what he really
fears is—to get well, even though in delirium he swears
most positively that this is not the case, and that, on the
contrary, he all too eagerly longs for his health. As for
this assurance, the more zealously it is made, the more
clearly is its double-mindedness revealed: that he desires

his health and yet does not will it, although he has it in his power. To desire what one cannot carry out is not such double-mindedness because the hindrance is not within the control of the one who desires it. But when the person who desires is himself the obstacle that keeps himself from getting his desire fulfilled, not by giving it up, for then he would be at one with himself, but both by not willing and yet by willing to continue to desire: then the double-mindedness is clear—if it can be made clear—or at least the fact is clear that it is double-mindedness. If what a man fears is not the mistake itself, but the reproach at being caught in the mistake, then that fear so far from helping him out of the error may even lead him into that which is still more ruinous, even if apart from this he had made no mistake.

So, too, with one who wishes to do good out of fear of punishment, if indeed it can be done in that fashion, if it is not as when the fear-ridden person turns his whole life into nothing but illness, out of fear of becoming ill. Fear of the punishment is so far from helping him to do the Good in truth, that it ruins him, just because punishment is a medicine. But everyone, even a child knows that nothing is so dangerous as a medicine—when it is used in the wrong way. Even if it does not end in death, it may bring on critical illness. And spiritually understood there is a ruinous illness, namely, *not to fear what a man should fear:* the sacredness of modesty, God in the heavens, the command of duty, the voice of conscience, the accountability to eternity. In order to be insured against or of being saved from this illness, it is profitable to a man that he should punish himself, "that he beat his breast and chastise his heart." It is still more fruitful that he be punished in order that the punishment may keep him awake and sober, for in whatever way this may be more precisely understood, it will be to his profit and his advantage; yes, truly to his advantage, if he voluntarily allows himself to be punished.

But then, in a spiritual sense, there is another illness, a still more destructive one: *to fear what a man should not and ought not to fear*. The first illness is defiance and obstinacy and willfullness. The second is cowardice and servility and hypocrisy. And this last is terrible just because it is an illness where the physician sees to his horror that the sick person has used the medicine—in the wrong way. It may indeed seem that the one that wills the Good out of fear of punishment may still not be called ill, for he really wills the Good. For surely punishment is not an illness? Yet he is none the less ill and his illness is just this: the confusing of the illness and the medicine. It might seem that the one who wills the Good out of fear of punishment cannot be said to have used the medicine, and therefore cannot be said to have used it wrongly. For he indeed wills the Good. He wishes to be healthy—out of his fear of having to use the medicine. But spiritually understood, where illness is not in the material body as the fever is in the blood, and where medicine is not something external, like drops in a bottle, then fear means: to use and to have used, to have taken the medicine—in the wrong way. This shows itself clearly in the terrible and fatal manifestations of that other illness.

It has been noted that fear of poverty suddenly makes the extravagant person miserly; but it is never observed that it makes him thrifty, and why not? Because the fear of the medicine lay in taking it in the wrong way. Indeed, fear of the body's infirmities has taught the voluptuary to observe moderation in debauchery (for the fear was to take the medicine in the wrong way) but it has never made him chaste. It taught him, instead of forgetting God

in the whirlpool of vice (sad distraction of mind!), daily
to mock God by moderation—in debauchery (abominable
discretion!). And indeed, fear of punishment has made
the sinner into a hypocrite, who in hypocrisy's loathesome
doubleness of mind pretended to love God (for the fear
was to take the medicine in the wrong way), but it has
never made him pure of heart. This is firmly established:
that punishment is not illness, but medicine. Thus it may
be a punishment for the frivolous person to be confined to
a sick bed, but suppose in truth he understands it as
punishment, then the illness, the fever or whatever other
disorder it now may be, then it is a medicine. On the other
hand, all double-mindedness that wills the Good only out
of fear of punishment can always be known in the end,
because it considers punishment as an illness. If double-
mindedness, then, which one may inwardly pity, is an
overtense anxiety, as when the horrified imagination of
the sick person alters the effect of the medicine: then the
mark is that punishment is confused with illness and one
who suffers from it simply does not in truth desire to
be released from the illness, but in falsity desires to be rid
of the medicine.

Now which is the punishment that is to be feared; what,
more precisely, is understood by it? When we reflect upon
that, double-mindedness becomes more obvious. For one
and the same illness may be regarded very differently and
its danger varies according to the different wrong concep-
tions of punishment that are present. *Someone may think
that by punishment is meant what is now seldom mentioned—the punishment of eternity.* And it might seem
that the person was not double-minded who wills the Good
out of fear of that punishment, since he refers the punishment to eternity, therefore to the same place where the
Good has its home. And yet, he does not will the Good,

he wills it only out of fear of punishment. Therefore—
if there were no punishment! In that "if" lurks double-
mindedness. If there were no punishment!! In that "if"
hisses double-mindedness. If there were no punishment, or
if indeed there was a man who could convince him that
eternity's punishment was a fantasy; or if it became common practice to think in this fashion; or if he could travel
to a foreign country where it was common practice; or
if cowardly and hypocritical superstition could discover
a cheap means of propitiation!!! Look at the double-
mindedness! Note that it can just as easily seek its consolation in unbelief as in superstition. And if double-
mindedness does not seek them out, then it is they that
try to capture double-mindedness until the matter becomes obvious. If one were briefly to characterize double-
mindedness by a single appropriate expression, what would
be more characteristic than that—"if," "in case that"!
For when the will in a man gets command so that he
keeps on willing the Good and in truth willing only that
one thing, then there is no "in case that." But double-
mindedness brings itself to a stop continually by its "in
case that." It does not contain the impetus of eternity and
does not have the infinite's open road before it. It passes
itself and meets itself as it is coming to a stop. It is said
that by the holy sign of the cross one can halt the evil
Spirit, so that it cannot go on. In this fashion, double-
mindedness brings itself to a halt by its pitiful sign, by its
"in case that." For a moment it may seem as if double-
mindedness did not exist. Double-mindedness can perhaps
speak in such a fashion that it deceives. But when a man
begins to act and there is double-mindedness in him, then
he is plunged immediately into this paralyzing "in case
that." It is true that a man may fill up the temporal order
with his talk, but eternity will reveal the nature of his

deeds. Only for him who wills the Good in truth, only for him can what is taught about the punishments of eternity be eternally true. The one that merely fears the punishment, for him it cannot remain eternally true, for there is nothing eternal in him, since the Eternal can only be in him if he wills the Good in truth. There is only one proof that the Eternal exists: faith in it.

Fear is a tottering proof, that proves that the fearful one does not believe or does so as when the devil believes, but trembles because he does not believe. Only one thing can help a man to will the Good in truth: the Good itself. Fear is a deceitful aid. It can embitter one's pleasure, make life laborious and miserable, make one old and decrepit; but it cannot help one to the Good since fear itself has a false conception of the Good—and the Good does not allow itself to be deceived. Or does not this also belong to the true nature of the Good, this zeal for itself, that will not tolerate anyone else, any strange helper, any interference by some contentious one who might only create confusion. For, when the Good took up its place at the goal where the reward beckons or where the Good itself beckons to a man, the Good against its will would then be forced to see and to put up with the fact that there were two paths, and two men bent on them; the one because he willed the Good in truth, and humbly but gladly followed its beckoning; the other because fear drove him thence. Spiritually understood, is it conceivable that two such different men could possibly be able to come to the same place! For in a spiritual sense, place is not something external, to which a slave might come against his will when the overseer uses his scourge. And the path is not something that does not matter whether one rides forwards or backwards. But the place and the path are within a man and just as the place is the blessed state of the striving soul, so the path is the striving soul's continual transformation. Nay, as the Good is only one thing, so it wishes also to be the only thing that aids a man. The Good suckles and nurses the infant, rears and nourishes the youth, strengthens the adult, supports the aged. The Good teaches the striving one. It helps him. But only in the way that the loving mother teaches a child to walk alone. The mother is far enough away from the child so that she cannot actually support the child, but she holds out her arms. She imitates the child's movements. If it totters she swiftly bends as if she would seize it—so the child believes that it is not walking alone. The most loving mother can do no more, if it be truly intended that the child shall walk alone. And yet she does more; for her face, her face, yes, it is beckoning like the reward of the Good and like the encouragement of Eternal Blessedness. So the child walks alone, with eyes fixed upon the mother's face, not on the difficulties of the way; supporting himself by the arms that do not hold on to him, striving after refuge in the mother's embrace, hardly suspecting that in the same moment he is proving that he can do without her, for now the child is walking alone. Fear, on the other hand, is a dry nurse for the child: it has no milk; a bloodless corrector for the youth: it has no beckoning encouragement; a niggardly disease for the adult: it has no blessing; a horror for the aged: when fear has to admit that the long painful time of schooling did not bring Eternal Blessedness.

Fear also wishes to help a man. It desires to teach him to walk alone, but not as a loving mother does it. For it is fear itself that continually upsets the child. It desires to help him forward, but not as a loving mother's beckoning. For it is fear itself that weighs him down so that he cannot move from the spot. It desires to lead him to the

goal, and yet it is the fear itself that makes the goal terrifying. It desires to help him to the Good, and yet that
kind of learner never wins the favor of the Good. Nor
does he ever become God's friend. For, as the Scriptures
teach, not only thieves and robbers, but also the fearful
may not enter into the kingdom of Heaven. The fearful
one desires Heaven not for itself. He desires it only out
of fear of punishment. Is not such a man double-minded
even though he was not one of those who would appear
wholly other than he was? Would not such a man be
double-minded if you saw him in his dreams, when in
sleep he has cast off the yoke of fear, when all is as he
would really have it be, and he is as he really is, as he
would be upon waking if fear did not exist? For it is
said of old that one learns to know a man's soul by his
dreams.[12]

If by the word punishment, one thinks of eternity's
punishment, it gives a false impression, as if indeed it were
not double-mindedness to will the Good only out of fear
of punishment. But yet this *is* double-mindedness. Even if
it happened to be a good man who in the agony of fear
preserved a certain slavish blamelessness out of fear of
punishment: still he is double-minded. *He does continually
what he really would rather not do,* or at least what he
has no pleasure in doing, for this pleasure is only a low
sensual pleasure, in fact of all sensual pleasures it is the
lowest. It is the one whose miserable glory consists solely
in avoiding something, hence the pleasure is not a pleasure
in itself, but only by contrast. *Nor does he attribute the
punishment to God and to the Good.* On the contrary, as
he pictures it, the Good is one thing, the punishment is
an entirely different matter. But in that case the Good is
not one thing. Thus by his double-mindedness he brings
about a strained relation between the Good and the pun-

ishment. He wishes that the punishment did not exist, and
thereby he really wishes also that the Good did not exist,
for otherwise he must have another relation to the Good
than the one that he has through punishment. Now punishment does exist, and so he performs the Good out of fear
of punishment. But the one that wills the Good in truth,
understands that punishment only exists for the sake of
the transgressors. He devoutly understands that punishment is like all other things which fall to the lot of one
who loves God. It is a helping hand. The double-minded
person shuns punishment as a suffering, a misfortune, an
evil, and thereby detaches himself and his understanding
from punishment, and wholly detaches punishment from
the Good. This obstinacy is like the infantile notion of a
child, who in his lack of judgment even sets up a cleft
in the father's nature; for the child imagines that the
father is the loving one, that punishment on the other
hand is something that a bad man has invented. That the
loving father himself should have invented the punishment
out of love for the child would not become apparent to
the child. So also with the relation between the Good and
punishment. It is the Good who, out of love for the pupil,
has invented punishment. We all go to school, only life's
school is for adults. For this reason the punishment is of
a more serious kind than in a children's school. It is less
obvious, and therefore all the more serious; less immediate,
and therefore all the more serious; less external, and there-
for all the more serious. It does not follow blow for blow
upon the mistake, and therefore all the more serious; one
has not been spared because it may seem as if the punishment had been forgotten, hence it is all the more serious.
Yet by this seriousness punishment does in truth press one
toward the Good, if one really wills it. Doubleness of mind
has no desire to do that. It continues to have an effeminate,

sensuous conception of punishment, and an impotent will
for the Good. It often happens with such a double-minded
person, that the older he gets the more impoverished his
life becomes: when his youth, in which there was something better than fear, is spent, and when fearfulness and
cleverness conspire together in order to make him into a
slave, if one wishes to put it so—to the Good. It is so
different with the one who wills the Good in truth. He
is the only one who is free, made free by the Good. However, a man does not in truth will the Good if he only
wills it out of fear of punishment, and hence is only in
a state of slavery to the Good.

*Yet double-mindedness seldom dwells on eternity's pun-
ishment. The punishment it fears is more often understood
in an earthly and temporal sense.* Of a man who only wills
the Good out of fear of punishment, it is necessary to
say with special emphasis, that he fears what a man should
not and ought not to fear: loss of money, loss of reputation, misjudgment by others, neglect, the world's judgment, the ridicule of fools, the laughter of the frivolous,
the cowardly whining of consideration, the inflated triviality of the moment, the fluttering mist-forms of vapor.
Yes, this double-minded man becomes as unsteady in all
his ways as the one who willed the Good for the sake of
the reward, because he is continually intent upon what
is in flux, upon what is always changing, and he fears
continually that which no man should fear. He fears
that which has power to wound, maltreat, ruin, or strike
dead the body, but which has no power whatever over
the soul unless it obtains it through fear. Should a man
love neither the earth, nor the pleasures of the eye, nor
the pleasures of the flesh, nor a haughty life; should he
covet neither what is the world's, the possession of money
and prestige among men, then he shall fear neither what

is the world's, neither the world nor men, neither poverty nor the expelling hand of persecution. If he fears these things, then he is the prey of double-mindedness, just as in this double-mindedness he is the slave of mankind.

Yes, there is a sense of shame, that is favorable to the Good. Woe to the man who casts it off! This sense of shame is a saving companion through life. Woe to the man that breaks with it! It is in the service of sanctification and of true freedom. Woe to the man who is scandalized by it as if it were a compulsion! If a man goes alone through life, according to the word of the Scriptures[13] that is not good, yet if he goes accompanied by that shame, oh, he shall become good and become one thing. And if the solitary one should stumble, if this sense of shame were still his companion, then we should not cry out as the book of Ecclesiastes does, "Woe to him that is alone," nor say of the solitary one, as does Ecclesiastes, "If he falls, who shall help him up."[14] For this sense of shame intends to serve him better than the best friend. It will help him better than all human sympathy which easily leads into double-mindedness—not into willing one thing. There is no question but what a man usually acts more intelligently, shows more strength, and to all appearances more self-control, when under the scrutiny of others than when he believes himself to be unobserved. But the question is whether this intelligence, this strength, this self-control is real, or whether through the devotion of long-continued attention to it, it does not easily slip into the lie of simulation which kindles the unsteady blush of double-mindedness in his soul. Each one who is not more ashamed before himself than before all others, if he is placed in difficulty and much tried in life, will in one way or another end by becoming the slave of men. For to be more ashamed in the presence of others than when alone, what else is this than to be more ashamed of seeming than of being? And turned about, should not a man be more ashamed of what he is than of what he seems? For otherwise he cannot in truth will one thing, since by trying to appear well in the eyes of others he is only striving after a changing shimmer and its reflection in human favor.

The clever one, who fears the judgment of others and is ashamed before others—if he is not ashamed most of all before himself, ah, perhaps his cunning might succeed in becoming undetectable, it might permit him to imagine that it was already unfathomable; and so, what then? This one who does not misuse his power because he fears the judgment of men and of being ashamed before men—if he is not ashamed most of all before himself, ah, perhaps either he himself or some eye-servant might even succeed in imagining that it could be done so craftily that not even God could see through it; and so, what then? Indeed it is unnecessary for the talk to wait for what will happen, that is, to wait for the outcome of his double-mindedness. For the talk is only about the presence of double-mindedness in him, and that is already obvious. Whether it becomes obvious to men or not, double-mindedness is none the less present, and the double-minded person is to be pitied. For let us not forget that truth is right in saying of each one who is in untruth, that he is indeed to be pitied, even when he himself and all men think him fortunate. Because, in the sense of truth, it does not help a man that he does not know that he is to be pitied, for this is only a further misfortune. But the one that is most ashamed of himself when he is alone, is thereby strengthened in willing one thing. However crafty this cunning may have been, the inventor himself can still see through it. Let it, then, be hidden from all men, no matter how its hiddenness might be able to support him, yet he could not hide it from that inner companion, before whom he is most of all ashamed.

We do not mean to imply here, that a man has ever lived, even in the most corrupt age, for whom no person existed whose judgment he might and could well fear with a wholesome shame, a person whose judgment could be a guide to him in order to will the Good in truth. But if this shame before the honored person is in truth to become a source of benefit to the humble man, then there is an indispensable condition: that the person must be ashamed most of all before himself. Therefore one could rightly say that in truth it is most beneficial of all to a man to feel shame before one who is already dead. And if he feels this humiliation before a living person, then to feel it before him as if he were already dead, or (if it seems more to your liking, my listener, I will use another expression, that means the same thing, although it contains the explanation in an aesthetic form): to feel ashamed before him as before a transfigured one. One already dead is just such a transfigured one. One who is living can indeed be mistaken, can be changed, can be stampeded in a moment and by the moment. If, in truth, he is a genuinely honorable person, he himself will, by way of warning, remind you of this in order that by your relationship with him you may not be led into that double-mindedness, which lies in being the follower of another. The living person may perhaps favor you too much —perhaps too little. If you see him each day, your shame will perhaps lose something of its intensity or perhaps bring on itself an acute disease, so that you could wish to possess a magic means of deceiving the revered one, so that you wished to be able to ingratiate yourself with him or by any means to raise yourself up in his good graces, because his judgment has become for you the most im-

portant thing of all. How much danger and temptation
to double-mindedness! It does not disappear until you
conduct yourself with him, as with one who is dead. Withdraw from him—but never forget him. That only leaves
when you are separated from him as though by death,
when in earthly or temporal fashion you do not come too
near him, but only forever remember what he himself
would have termed the best thing in his nature! A man
cannot get round a transfigured one. Favor and persuasion
and overhastiness belong to the moments of earthly life.
The departed one does not notice these appearances, the
transfigured one cannot understand them. He does not
wish to understand them.

If you will not give them up, then you must give him
up; then you must, if you dare, offend the transfigured
one, break with him, yes, annihilate him. For when he
is not the transfigured one, then he simply does not exist.
With the living one, you may speak in another manner,
because he also exists in the earthly sense, and if you get
him changed a little—alas, to what other end than to
your own destruction and to his disparagement! It would
be as if you still had him to hold to, you had his words,
his audible approval, and in the union between you two
perhaps it would escape you both that a change had taken
place. But the transfigured one exists only as transfigured,
not visibly to the earthly eye, not audibly to the earthly
ear, only in the sacredly still silence of shame. He cannot
be changed, not in the least particular, without its being
instantly noted, and without all being lost, and without
his vanishing. The transfigured one exists only as transfigured. He cannot be changed into anything better. He
is the transfigured one. He cannot be altered. He is indeed
a departed one. He remains true to himself, one and the
same—this glorified one! How, then, could it be possible

for one to become double-minded who by feeling ashamed
before such a one is strengthened in willing the Good!
However, even the most upright man can nevertheless be
surprised by many frailties and occasionally may go astray.
But then he has a hope: that there exists a God, a just
government of the universe, that by punishment will
awaken him and lead him back. How different it is! He
that wills the Good in truth even hopes for the punishment; but that man who in his double-mindedness only
wills the Good out of fear of punishment is far from willing
the Good in truth.

The double-minded person stands at a parting of the
ways, where two visions appear: the Good and the terrifying figure of punishment. The two do not belong together in his eyes, for while punishment, which God in
His wisdom has connected with every transgression, is a
Good, there is no denying that it is such a Good only when
it is gratefully received, not when it is simply feared as
an evil. But the double-minded person rarely has this Divine punishment in mind. He thinks rather of the world's
punishment. But the Good and the punishment the world
metes out are not identical. Or has the world perhaps really
become so perfect and so holy, that it is like God, and
that what it rewards is the Good and what it punishes, the
evil? Or would any person who believes that he has received at God's hand an intimation of the life according
to which he desires to model his own life, could such a
man really think of worshiping the world in this way?
To be sure, one may hear—especially in the places where
men festively gather in order to deceive one another by
many speeches—one may hear magnificent words about
how the world progresses, and about our age and about
our century. But, my listener, would you dare, as a father
(and I feel confident that you have a lofty conception of

the meaning of this name, a responsible conception of the
charge which it lays upon you) would you dare, as a
father, to say to your child as you sent him out into the
world, "Go, with your mind at ease, my child, pay attention to what the many approve and what the world
rewards, for that is the Good, but what the world punishes, that is evil. It is no longer true as it used to be, that
the judgment of the masses is like foam on water—nonsense, though loudly proclaimed; blind, though sharply
decisive; impossible to follow because it changes more
swiftly than a woman changes color. Now, there is no
longer any doubt about the outcome, the Good is immediately victorious. Now, the Good exacts no sacrifice,
no self-denial, for the world desires the Good. Now, the
judgment of the masses is the judgment of the wise men,
the solitary ones are the fools. Now, the earth is the
kingdom of God, and Heaven is only a reflection of it.
Now, the world is the highest certainty, the only one a
man can build upon, the only one a man can swear by."

Surely, my listener, the speech need not ask you, for it
rests assured in advance what your answer would be. But
I would like to ask of the most ardent attender of those
festivities: would you dare, if you should speak as a father
to your own child, would you dare say any such thing?
Or if it were the youth that, with all the earnest devotion
of his soul, fixed his trusting gaze on you, assured that if
you said it, it must be so, and in gratitude, bound by a
solemn vow to follow the guidance of your counsel
through life; would you dare give him any such counsel?
Or if you were witness to that lovable young man's beautiful enthusiasm when he read and heard of the great men
who fought with a heavy destiny and suffered badly in
the world, the glorious ones whom earth renounced because it was not worthy of them, would you dare, when

no clamor caused your speech to wander but when the stillness of intimacy, of the lovable one's confidence, the inexperience of the young man, all obliged you to tell the truth; at such a time would you dare lay your hand on your heart and say, "Such things no longer happen. Now the world has become enlightened and perfect. Now: to seek first after this world and its customs is identical with what was meant in former times by seeking first God's kingdom and His righteousness."

Alas, gradually as a man gets older, he grows accustomed to a great deal in life. Among other things, he gets in the habit of saying much that he has not properly reflected upon. Among contemporaries he gets into the way of hedging round what he says by so many presuppositions that that which is plain and elevating is almost forgotten. Now and then a word is let drop that expresses a plain and solid exasperation of long standing, "You know well enough what kind of world we live in." And at other times the world is praised to the point of idolatry, without either of these statements making any very deep impression on the one who speaks them. For the first does not arouse him. It does not frighten him into a condition of fear and trembling in which he resolves to save himself since the world is so bad. And the other does not strengthen the speaker into an eager desire for the Good by confidence in the perfection of the world. Alas, along with others in this life, he gets accustomed, amid the dull round of habit, almost to abandon himself as he plays about with mere words.

But when even the most tragic of life's spoiled children seriously admonishes a child, a youth, a maiden, he speaks with shame. There is at this point a beautiful reciprocity, for the youth approaches his elder with shame and the elder in admonishing the youth always speaks with shame.

May God grant that all who have an opportunity to admonish youth may themselves derive some benefit from the shame which comes with the admonishment!

In the act of admonishing, and this deserves emphasis, the older person shall by no means set before the youth a horrifying picture of the world. To do so is never earnestness, but is only sickly imagination. But in the act of admonishing, he will shrink before the thought of leading the youth straight into the danger of double-mindedness by deceptively focusing his attention upon the punishment the world metes out. For in this, instead of impressing upon him a holy fear and shame before the Good, he is polluting the pure one by teaching him the fear of loss of money, loss of reputation, misjudgment by others, neglect, the world's judgment, the ridicule of fools, the laughter of the frivolous, the cowardly whining of consideration, the inflated triviality of the moment, the fluttering mist-forms of vapor. Alas, for many men these elevated thoughts are only too often like a gilding, that wears off in life's double-mindedness, which gnaws and gnaws. But even the man whom double-mindedness has eaten most bare, when he speaks admonishingly to a youth, is reminded that, out of shame, he dare say but one thing. In the act of admonishing even he will say (for it is no rare speaker that is here introduced to talk, and just on that account the praise of the Good is so much the more glorious because it does not require the approval of eloquence, for here it is well to note that it is one of life's most tragically spoiled children who speaks admonishingly to a youth) even he will say, "Do not be afraid, be slow to judge others, but attend closely to yourself, hold firmly to willing one thing, to willing the Good in truth, and thus, from now on, let this lead you wherever for now it will lead you—because eternally it will lead you to victory.

In this world let it lead you to prosperity or poverty, to honor or insult, to life or death: only do not let go this one thing. By its hand you may walk confidently even in danger. Even in danger of your life itself you may go as confidently as a child who clasps the mother's hand. Yes, even more confidently, for the child does not even know the danger." In the act of admonishing, therefore, a man should warn against fear of the world's punishment, which is double-mindedness.

Now and then someone speaks of "suffering punishment, when one does the Good." How is that possible? From whom shall that punishment come? Certainly not from God! Is it, then, from the world—so that when in its wisdom the world is mistaken, it rewards the bad and punishes the Good? And yet no, it is not as that word "world" implies. The word does not mean what it says. It is improperly expressed. For the word "world" sounds great and terrifying, and yet it must obey the same law as the most insignificant and miserable man. But even if the world gathered all its strength, there is one thing it is not able to do, it can no more punish an innocent one than it can put a dead person to death.

To be sure the world has power. It can lay many a burden upon the innocent one. It can make his life sour and laborious for him. It can rob him of his life. But it cannot punish an innocent one. How wonderful, here is a limit, a limit that is invisible, like a line that is easy to overlook with the senses, but one that has the strength of eternity in resisting any infringement. This may be overlooked by the world whose attention is focused upon that which is big—and the limit is insignificant, is for the present, a quiet-mannered nobody, but yet it is there. Perhaps it is completely hidden from the eyes of the world. For that, too, can be a part of the innocent one's suffering, that the world's injustice takes on the appearance of punishment—in the world's eyes. But the limit is nevertheless there, and is in spite of all the strongest. And even if all the world rose up in tumult and even if everything were thrown into confusion: the limit is nevertheless there. And on the one side of it with the innocent ones is justice; and on the other side toward the world is an eternal impossibility of punishing an innocent one. Even if the world wishes to annihilate an innocent man and put him out of the way, it cannot put the limit out of the way, even though it be invisible. (Perhaps it is just on that account.) Even in the moment of his sacrificial death, the limit is there: then it stretches itself with the strength of eternity, then it cleaves itself with eternity's all-encompassing depth. The limit is there, and on the one side with the innocent ones is justice, and on the other side toward the world is an eternal impossibility of punishing an innocent one.

When the good man truly stands on the other side of the boundary line inside the fortification of eternity, he is strong, stronger than the whole world. He is strongest of all at the time when he seems to be overcome. But the impotent double-minded one has removed the boundary limit, because he only wills the Good out of fear of earth's punishment. If the world is not really the land of perfection, then by his double-mindedness he has surrendered himself to the power of mediocrity or pledged himself to the evil.

6. Barriers to Willing One Thing:
Egocentric Service of the Good

3. *Furthermore it must be said that the man who wills
the Good and wills its victory out of a self-centered
willfullness does not will one thing. He is double-minded.*

SUPPOSE A MAN wills the Good simply in order
that *he* may score the victory, then he wills the Good for
the sake of the reward, and his double-mindedness is obvious, as the previous section of the talk has sought to
point out. Actually he does not care to serve the Good,
but to have the advantage of regarding it as a fruit of
conquest. When, on the contrary, a man desires that the
Good shall be victorious, when he will not call the outcome of the battle "victory," if *he* wins, but only when
the Good is victorious: can he then, in any sense, be called
and be double-minded? Yes, and yet if he be double-
minded (for the decision as to the boundary line between
the pure and the double-minded is here of a singular com-
plexity), then his double-mindedness is more subtle and
concealed, more presumptuous than that obvious and out-
and-out worldly sort. It is a powerful deception that seems
nearest of all to approach the purity of heart that wills
the Good in truth, even though it is at the other pole
from it, just as the high place is from the deep chasm,
just as heaven-storming pride is from humility's dwelling
in the low places, just as if a pretentiously plausible ap-
proximation had been won by falsifying a line of separation that was eternally real. He does not will the Good

for the sake of the reward. He wills that the Good shall triumph through *him*, that he shall be the instrument, he the chosen one. He does not desire to be rewarded by the world—that he despises; nor by men—that he looks down upon. And yet he does not wish to be an unprofitable servant.[15] The reward which he insists upon is a sense of pride and in that very demand is his violent double-mindedness. Yes, violent, for what else does he wish than to take the Good by storm, and by force to press himself and his service upon the Good! And if he will not give up this last presumptuousness, if he, in some way, does not desire what the Good wills, if he does not desire the Good's victory after the fashion that the Good wills it: then he is double-minded. Even if he knows how to hide it from men, even if he hides it from himself, even if the true expression of the language seems for a moment to hide it by calling his condition of mind self-will, willfullness, for that sounds well, especially when it is strong enough to venture the most extreme things: does that seem to be double-mindedness? No, it does not seem to be double-mindedness, but it is.

In the eyes of this double-minded person the Good is one thing, its victory is another, and its victory through him may even be something else. Now it is indeed the case, that eternally the Good has always been victorious. But in time it is otherwise, temporally it may take a long time. The victory is slow, its uncertainty is a slow measure of length. Again and again the faithful servant's life ends, and it seemed, at his death, as if he had accomplished nothing for the Good. And yet he was a faithful servant, who willed the Good in truth, and he was also loved by the Good, that prizes obedience more than the "fat of the ram." "Alas, why does time exist; if the Good eternally has always been victorious, why should it then creep

slowly forward throughout the length of time or almost
perish in time's slowness? Why should it fight laboriously
through that which makes time the longest, through uncertainty? Why should the solitary 'individuals,'[16] who
sincerely will the Good, be so scattered, so separated, that
they can scarcely call out to one another, scarcely catch
sight of one another? Why should time hang like a weight
upon them? Why should separation involve them in delay,
when it is so swiftly accomplished in eternity? Why was
an immortal spirit placed in the world and in time, just as
the fish is drawn up out of the water and cast upon the
beach?" Whoever talks in this questioning vein (and even
if he say it amid groans, the utterance is the same), should
be on his guard, for he scarcely knows by what spirit he is
speaking. Alas, men often enough confuse impatience with
humble, obedient enthusiasm; impatience even lends itself
to this confusion. When a man is active early and late
"for the sake of the Good," storming about noisily and
restlessly, hurling himself into time, as a sick man throws
himself down upon his bed, throwing off all consideration
for himself, as a sick man throws off his clothes, scornful
of the world's reward; when such a man makes a place
among men, then the masses think what he himself imagines, that he is inspired. And yet he is at the other pole
from that, for he is double-minded, and double-mindedness no more resembles inspiration than a whirlwind resembles the steadiness of the standing wind.

So it is with all impatience. It is a kind of ill-temper.
Its root is already in the child, because the child will not
take time for things. With the double-minded one, it is
thus clear that time and eternity cannot rule in the same
man. He cannot, he will not, understand the Good's
slowness; that out of mercy, the Good is slow; that out
of love for free persons, it will not use force; that in its

wisdom toward the frail ones, it shrinks from any deception. He cannot, he will not, humbly understand that
the Good can get on without him. He is double-minded,
he that with his enthusiasm could apparently become an
apostle, but can quite as readily become a Judas, who
treacherously wishes to hasten the victory of the Good.
He is scandalized, he that by his enthusiasm seems to love
the Good so highly. He is scandalized by its poverty, when
it is clothed in the slowness of time. He is not devoted to
the Good in service that may profit nothing. He only
effervesces, and he that effervesces loves the moment. And
he that loves the moment fears time, he fears that the
course of time will reveal his double-mindedness, and he
falsifies eternity; for otherwise eternity might still more
effectively reveal his double-mindedness. He is a falsifier.
For him eternity is the deceptive sensory illusion of the
horizon; for him eternity is the bluish haze that limits
time; for him eternity is the dazzling sleight-of-hand trick
executed by the moment.

Such a double-minded person is perhaps hardly recognizable in this world, because his double-mindedness is
not evident inside the world. The world's reward and
punishment do not serve as informers against him; for
he has overcome the world, even if by a higher deception.
Hence his double-mindedness is first recognizable at the
boundary where time and eternity touch upon each other.
There it is clear and is always recognized by the all-
knowing One. He will not be content with the blessed
assurance which comforts beyond all measure: that eternally the Good has always been victorious; the blessed
assurance which is a security that passeth all understanding; the blessed assurance that the unprofitable servant
may have within himself at each moment, even when the
time is the longest and he seems to have accomplished least

of all, the blessed assurance which allows the unprofitable servant if he loses honor to speak more proudly than that royal word: All is lost save honor.[17] And when even honor is lost to say: Nothing is lost, but all is gained.

But this double-minded person is not so easily recognizable on earth. He does not will the Good for the sake of reward, for then he would have become obvious in his aspiration or in his despair. He does not will the Good out of fear of punishment, for then he would have become obvious in his cowardice, in his shunning of punishment, or in his despair, when he was not able to avoid it. No, he wishes to sacrifice all, he fears nothing, only he will not sacrifice himself in daily self-forgetfulness. This he fears to do.

The double-minded man stands at a parting of the ways, and sees there two apparitions: the Good, and the Good in its victory, or even in its victory through him. This latter is presumptuousness, but even the first two apparitions are not wholly the same. In eternity they are the same, but not in time. And they must be kept apart. The Good so wills it. The Good puts on the slowness of time as a poor garment, and in keeping with this change of dress one who serves it must be clothed in the insignificant figure of the unprofitable servant. With the eye of his senses he is not permitted to see the Good in victory. Only with the eye of faith can he strive after its eternal victory. Therein lies his double-mindedness. For as there is a double-mindedness which divides up the nature of the Good which the Good has united for all eternity: so is his double-mindedness of that sort that unites what the Good in time has set apart. The one double-minded person forgets the Eternal and on that account misuses time, the other misuses eternity.

7. Barriers to Willing One Thing:
Commitment to a Certain Degree

4. Before finally leaving the subject of double-mindedness
for a similar examination of purity, *the talk should at
least touch upon that versatile form of double-mindedness: the double-mindedness of weakness* as it appears
in the common things of real life; *upon the fact that
the person who only wills the Good up to a certain
degree is double-minded.*

At bottom this is the way all double-mind-
edness expresses itself in relation to the Good, in that it
wills the Good only up to a certain degree. But what has
been set forth above, what of double-mindedness might
perhaps be spoken of as its deceptive transactions in the
"big," still had a certain semblance of unity, and of inner
consistency, in so far as it was one single thing that was
betrayed into one-sidedness, yet this one-sidedness, however strange it may seem, was precisely the double-mindedness in that one-sided person.

It is otherwise with the transactions of daily life, for
they are not in the "big." It is rare in daily life, to see
anyone who wills some perverse thing with fixed consistency and effort. The transactions of daily life are made
in the little things so that double-mindedness presents a
much greater diversity within the "individual."

A merchant who deals in only one kind of ware is a
rare sight, and so is that double-mindedness which has a
certain unreal unity. A merchant generally deals in dif-

ferent wares, and double-mindedness, too, is generally a number of different things. On that account the false road is harder to detect than that clear-cut one. Nay, the false roads cross each other and the right road in the most different ways and the "individual" shares in this crossing in an equally varied way. To be sure his life is distinguishable as falling within double-mindedness. But it is not easy to designate it any more closely, because within this double-mindedness, he is not at one with himself in anything definite, but is tossed about in vacillation by every breeze. For he learns and learns and yet never comes to a knowledge of truth.[18] Or if he comes almost to it, then he quickly turns further and further away the more he learns of this confused and confusing instruction. In preference to the earlier double-mindedness, this has the Good on its side, in that it wills the Good, even though weakly; and in that it is without the obstinacy that marked the previously mentioned double-mindedness. But upon occasion weakness may be just as incurable.

This double-mindedness is difficult to speak of because it approximates both the one and the other, and because it alters itself continually, changing so swiftly that it may have transformed itself several times before the talk had hardly finished describing a single expression. It plays about gaily not only in all possible colors, but there is not even any law for this play of colors that blends colors and color relations in ever new confusion. Hence there is always something new under the sun—and yet the old double-mindedness persists. Indeed what makes it even more difficult to speak of, is that in daily life, where it is right at home, double-mindedness, within limits, keeps comparatively to itself, so that a double-minded person, by being a little less double-minded than the others, claims distinction even though his degree of difference is quite

within an essential sameness. Hence in the end it would
seem as if that true eternal claim that demands purity of
heart, by willing one thing, were done away with, as if
it had been withdrawn from government, set away in retirement at such a distance from daily life that there
simply could be no talk about it. For among the many-
colored seething populace in the noise of the world from
day to day and from year to year, there is no scrupulous
check made as to whether a person wholly wills the Good
if he has influence and might, runs a great business, is
something in his own and in others' eyes. "What fright-
fully niggardly pettiness," one thinks, "to be so scrupulous!" One does not consider that there is any presumptuousness in what one has spoken. Nay, one drops the
clever remark in passing and hurries on, while the remark
also hurries on from mouth to mouth amid the many-
colored seething populace. And in the rush of life, in trade
and commerce from morning to night, there is no such
scruple about whether a person wholly wills the Good,
just so that in his business he is keen, not to say a "thief,"
just so that he saves and piles up money, just so that he
has a good reputation and by good fortune manages to
avoid slander (for whether he actually is guilty or not is
here of little importance, for neither he nor the world has
time to look into that. Slander is merely a danger as an
obstacle to his business). "To what purpose such a delay
in the midst of busyness?" And in the world, it is always
busy. Yes, it is entirely true that this is the way things
look in the world, the way they seem in the world, and
the way they must seem within the deceptive horizon of
the temporal order. But in eternity it will make a tre-
mendous difference whether a person was scrupulous or
not.

And yet eternity is not like a new world, so that one

who had lived in time according to the ways of the time world and of the press of busyness, if he were to make a happy landing in eternity itself, could now try his luck in adopting the customs and practices of eternity. Alas, the temporal order and the press of busyness believe, that eternity is so far away. And yet not even the foremost professional theatrical producer has ever had all in such readiness for the stage and for the change of scenes, as eternity has all in readiness for time: all—even to the least detail, even to the most insignificant word that is spoken; has all in readiness in each instant—although eternity delays.

Oh, that this talk, far from detaining anyone who sincerely wills the Good, or calling anyone away from fruitful activity, might cause a busy man to pause. For this press of busyness is like a charm. And it is sad to observe how its power swells, how it reaches out seeking always to lay hold of ever-younger victims so that childhood or youth are scarcely allowed the quiet and the retirement in which the Eternal may unfold a divine growth. And suppose that busyness in its haste should make a concession, believing even in its superficial wisdom that there is something beneficial in having a busy man on hand who now and then hurriedly proclaims that higher reflection on life about willing the Good in truth. Alas, is this, then, the true relationship? Are almost all to be excused from that which every man should do for himself? But then for the sake of completeness is someone in the midst of busyness to be delegated the task of setting forth that higher claim—that higher claim, which, if by some means it could be satisfied, even if in feebleness and in imperfection, would command a man's whole mind, his unrelenting industry, his best strength?

Thus in the midst of busyness, double-mindedness is to

be found. Just as the echo dwells in the woods, as stillness dwells in the desert, so double-mindedness dwells in the press of busyness. That the one who wills the Good only to a certain degree, that he is double-minded, that he has a distracted mind, a divided heart, scarcely needs to be pointed out. But the reason may need to be explained and set forth, why, in the press of busyness, there is neither time nor quiet to win the transparency that is indispensable if a man is to come to understand himself in willing one thing or even for a preliminary understanding of himself in his confusion. Nay, the press of busyness into which one steadily enters further and further, and the noise in which the truth continually slips more and more into oblivion, and the mass of connections, stimuli, and hindrances, these make it ever more impossible for one to win any deeper knowledge of himself. It is true, that a mirror has the quality of enabling a man to see his image in it, but for this he must stand still. If he rushes hastily by, then he sees nothing. Suppose a man should go about with a mirror in his possession which he does not take out, how should such a man get to see himself? In this fashion the busy man hurries on, with the possibility of understanding himself in his possession. But the busy man keeps on running and it never dawns upon him that this possibility which he has in his possession is rapidly fading from his memory. And yet one hardly dares say this to one of these busy ones, for however rushed he otherwise may be, yet upon occasion he has plenty of time for a multitude of excuses by the use of which he becomes worse than he was before: excuses whose wisdom is about the same as when a sailor believes that it is the sea, not the ship, that is moving.

One hardly dares say this to him, for however rushed he otherwise may be, yet upon occasion when in the company of congenial spirits, he has ample time: "to rob the unripe fruit of ridicule of its wisdom," in order to poke fun at the speaker as one of life's incompetents, as a man whom the busy one in his cleverness ignores—from the exalted viewpoint of his excuses. Then, too, the general approval is everywhere upon the side of the busy one—everywhere, in the ever-increasing sum of the pressure of busyness, and in the swarming mass of excuses. For like a poisonous breath over the fields, like a mass of locusts over Egypt, so the swarm of excuses is a general plague, a ruinous infection among men, that eats off the sprouts of the Eternal. For with each one who is attacked, there is always just one more excuse for the next person. And while a person cannot, as a rule, prevent a sickness becoming more and more dangerous, more and more malignant, the more it attacks those around him, yet with excuses it is just the reverse. There the sickness seems to become milder and milder, the condition becomes more and more agreeable, the more persons there are attacked by it. And if we all agree that the wretched, stunted state of health of these excuses, is the highest of all, then there is no one to say anything to the contrary. Should there be an "individual" who could not feel easy about yielding, and who raised a strong objection to this widespread practice of excusing, alas, we have not yet heard all; for there is always one excuse held in reserve, that lies in wait at his door and demands of him, "What good does it do for a single individual to insist upon opposing this?" Hence once again with excuses it is even worse than with a virulent disease, for no one dies of a disease simply because others have died of it.

So the double-minded person, then, may have a feeling —a living feeling for the Good. If someone should speak of the Good, especially if it were done in a poetical fashion,

then he is quickly moved, easily stimulated to melt away
in emotion. Suppose the world goes a little against him
and then someone should tell him that God is love, that
His love surpasses all understanding, encompassing in His
Providence even the sparrow that may not fall to the earth
without His willing it. If a person speaks in this way,
especially in a poetical manner, he is gripped. He reaches
after faith as after a desire, and with faith he clutches
for the desired help. In the faith of this desire he then
has a feeling for the Good. But perhaps the help is de-
layed. Instead of it a sufferer comes to him whom he can
help. But this sufferer finds him impatient, forbidding.
This sufferer must be content with the excuse, "that he
is not at the moment in the spirit or the mood to concern
himself about the sufferings of others as he himself has
troubles." And yet he imagines that he has faith, faith
that there is a loving Providence who helps the sufferer,
a Providence, who also uses men as his instruments. Possibly now the desired help comes. Again he quickly flares
up with gratitude, basking in a soft conception of the
loving Goodness of Providence. Now he thinks he has
rightly grasped faith. Now it has been victorious in him
over every doubt and every objection. Alas, and that other
sufferer has been completely forgotten. What else is this
condition if it is not double-mindedness! For suppose, after
all, that there should be talk of objections to faith, of
incidents and occurrences that seem as it were to cry out
against the care of a loving Providence: then that other
sufferer who with the excuse that by chance he was not
in the mood was turned away sharply by the very one
who could have helped him, that other sufferer is an even
more powerful objection. But the double-minded one is
wholly blind to the fact that at the very moment when
he believes faith to have conquered in him, he has, pre-

cisely by his action, refuted this conviction. Or is this
not double-mindedness that thinks to have a conviction
while by his own action a man contradicts it? Is this not,
in truth, the sole proof that a man has a conviction: that
his own life actually expresses it? Is this not the sole certainty: that one's so-called conviction is not altered from
moment to moment as a result of the different things that
happen to one, things that momentarily alter a person and
alter everything for a person so that today he has faith,
and tomorrow he has lost it, and he gets it again day after
tomorrow until something completely out of the ordinary
happens, at which time he almost inevitably loses it, assuming that he has ever had it!

Suppose that there were two men: a double-minded
man, who believes he has gained faith in a loving Providence, because he had himself experienced having been
helped, even though he had hardheartedly sent away a
sufferer whom he could have helped; and another man
whose life, by devoted love, was an instrument in the
hand of Providence, so that he helped many suffering ones,
although the help he himself had wished continued to
be denied him from year to year. Which of these two was
in truth convinced that there is a loving Providence that
cares for the suffering ones? Is it not a fair and a convincing conclusion: He that planted the ear, shall he not
hear.[19] But turn it around, and is the conclusion not
equally fair and convincing: He whose life is sacrificing
love shall he not trust that God is love? Yet in the press
of busyness there is neither time nor quiet for the calm
transparency which teaches equality, which teaches the
willingness to pull in the same yoke with other men, that
noble simplicity, that is in inner understanding with every
man. There is neither time nor quiet to win such a conviction. Therefore, in the press of busyness even faith

and hope and love and willing the Good become only loose
words and double-mindedness. Or is it not double-mindedness to live without any conviction, or more rightly, to
live in the constantly and continually changing fantasy
that one has and that one has not a conviction!

In this fashion feeling deceives the busy one into double-
mindedness. Perhaps after the flaming up of the contrition
of repentance, if this turns into emptiness, he had a conviction, at least so he believed, that there is a mercy that
forgives sins. But even in the forgiveness he strongly
denied any implication that he had been guilty of anything. Hence he had, so he thought, believed in a conviction that such a mercy exists, and yet in practice he denied
its existence; in practice his attitude seemed designed to
prove that it did not exist. Suppose that there were two
men, that double-minded one, and then another man who
would gladly forgive his debtor, if he himself might only
find mercy. Which of these two was in truth convinced
that such a mercy exists? The latter had indeed this proof
that it exists, that he himself practices it, the former has
no proof at all for himself, and only meets the contrary
proof which he himself presents. Or the double-minded
one perhaps had a feeling for right and wrong. It blazed
strongly in him, especially if someone would describe in a
poetical manner the zealous men, who by self-sacrifice in
the service of truth, maintained righteousness and justice.
Then some wrong happened to this man himself. And then
it seemed to him as if there must appear some sign in heaven
and upon earth since the world order could no more sleep
than he until this wrong was put right again. And this
was not self-love that inflamed him, but it was a feeling for
justice, so he thought. And when he obtained his rights,
no matter how much wrong it had cost those around him,
then once again he praised the perfection of the world.

Feeling had indeed carried him away, but also it had so enraptured him that he had forgotten the most important of all: to support righteousness and justice with self-sacrifice in the service of the truth. For which of these two is really convinced that justice exists in the world: the one that suffers wrong for doing the right, or the one that does wrong in order to obtain his right?

The immediate feeling is indeed—primary. It is the *élan vital* out of which life flows, just as it is said that the heart is the source of life. But then this feeling must be "kept," understood in the sense that one says, "Keep thy heart with all diligence, for out of it are the issues of life."[20] It must be cleansed of selfishness, kept from selfishness. It must not be delivered up to its own devices. On the other hand, that which will be kept must always put its trust in a higher power who will keep it; hence, even the loving mother begs God to keep her child.

In immediate feeling one man never understands another. As soon as something happens to himself, all things seem different to him. When he himself suffers he does not understand the suffering of another and neither is his own happiness the key to understand the happiness of another. The immediate feeling selfishly understands all in relation to itself, and is therefore in the discord of double-mindedness with all others. For only in the well-understood equality of sincerity can there be unity, and in selfish shortsightedness his conviction is continually being altered. If it is not altered it is an accident, since the cause of its exemption is only that by sheer chance his life was not touched by any change. But the stability of such a conviction is mere fantasy on the part of the one whom fate has pampered. Because a conviction is not firmly fixed when all press upon it equally and hold it firm. Rather, its true stability is revealed when everything is changed. It is rare indeed that a man's life is able to escape all changes, and in the changes the conviction based on immediate feeling is a fantasy, the momentary impression simply inflated into a consideration of the whole life.

Perhaps the double-minded one had a knowledge of the Good. In the moment of contemplation it stood out so distinctly before him, so clearly, that the Good, in truth, has all the advantage on its side, that the Good, in truth, is a gain both for this and for the future life. Yes, it lay on his heart, as though he must be able to convince the whole world of it. Perhaps it was not demanded of him that he should go out with his acquired conviction in order to convince others, but the testing that should try this newly won conviction nevertheless was not left out. Alas, contemplation and the moment of contemplation, in spite of all their clarity, readily conceal a deception; because the moment of contemplation has something in common with the falsified eternity. It is a foreshortening that is neces- sary in order that the contemplation may take place. It must foreshorten time a good deal. Indeed it must actually call the senses and thoughts away from time in order that they may complete themselves in a spurious eternal well- roundedness. It is here as when an artist sketches a country. The sketch cannot be as big as the country, it must be in- finitely smaller; but on that account it also becomes all the easier for the observer to scan the outlines of that country. And yet it may well happen to the observer, if suddenly he were actually set down in that country where the many, many miles really exist and are valid, that he would be unable to recognize the country, or to make any sense of it, or as a traveler, to find his way about in it. So it will be with the double-minded person. His knowledge has in- deed been a sense-deception. What was there, in air-tight fashion pressed together in the completeness of contempla-

tion, shall now be stretched out at its full length. It is now
no longer rounded off but is in motion. For life is like a
poet, and on that account is different from the observer
who always seeks to bring things to a conclusion. The poet
pulls us into the very complex center of life.

Now the double-minded person stands there with contemplation's sketch. Time, that was ignored by contemplation, begins to assert its validity. And it is obvious that in
all eternity, time has no right to deny that the Good has
all the advantage on its side. But it has permission to stretch
time out, and thereby to make somewhat more difficult
what in contemplation is apparently so plainly understood.
So the understanding does not, in this way, simply become
less plain because it has become crooked and awry, but
rather it has become less plain—to go by. Now instead
of keeping his contemplation to himself and holding himself to the contemplation in order to penetrate time with
it in a direct but gradual manner, the double-minded person lets time cut him off from contemplation. Is this not
double-mindedness: to be in time without any contemplation, without any distinct thoughts, or to put it more exactly, to be within time deceived over and over again about
having or having had an experience of contemplation! The
moment of contemplation he had recklessly misunderstood
as being earnest, and then as this earnestness really ap-
proached, he threw off contemplation, and misunderstood
the moment of contemplation as a delusion, until he again
becomes earnest in the moment of contemplation. Or perhaps the double-minded one himself admitted that he had
done wrong, had acted badly, had gotten upon a false
road. But then after reflection it became so evident, so at-
tractive, that punishment really is like a medicine. It
seemed to him that no physician had ever made his medicine so agreeable or inviting, as this reflection upon punish-

ment had succeeded in rendering it. However, when the
punishment came, momentarily, as a physician knows, it
made the condition worse, in order that real health might
break through. Then he became impatient. In reflection he
had thought himself healed; thought how good it was,
when it was all over—when it was all over. In this fashion
the lazy man always has a disproportionate power of imagination. He thinks immediately how he will establish himself, and how fine it will be for him when now this and
now that is done: he is less given to thinking—that he
should do this and that. And in reflection this looks very
inviting, but when he must step out upon the road (for
reflection is up above the road) then all is changed. Now
instead of keeping the reflection and the estimate to himself, and conforming to them, he throws off reflection.
He has lightly taken the reflection in vain, as if it were
the healing quality of the medicine, and as the healing is
about to begin, he light-mindedly misunderstands the reflection as a delusion. Is this not double-mindedness: to be
ill, to put oneself under the physician's treatment, and yet
not be willing to trust the physician, but arbitrarily to
break off the treatment! Is this not double-mindedness,
when the sick person is perhaps getting into the bath,
where the heat increases, but now finding it suddenly too
warm he springs out, regardless of all danger! Is it not
double-mindedness, when he still has a remnant of deliberation left and with it an intimation that actually he is
ill and so he begins to go through his cure all over again
—in the same fashion!

In the recognition, that contemplation and reflection are
the distance of eternity away from time and actuality,
there is indeed a truth: the knower can understand that
truth, but he cannot understand himself. It is certain that
without this recognition a man's life is more or less thought-

less. But it is also certain, that this recognition, because it is in a spurious eternity before the imagination, develops double-mindedness, if it is not slowly and honestly earned by the will's purity.

So the double-minded person may have had a will to the Good, for the one who is betrayed into double-mindedness by feeling, or by that distant recognition, he too has a will; but it received no power, and the germ of double-mindedness lay in the inner psychical disagreement. He also has a will to the Good. He is not without intentions or purposes, and resolutions and plans for himself, and not without plans of participation for others. But he has left something out: namely, he does not believe that the will in itself is, or indeed should be, the most solid of all, that it should be as hard as the sword that could hew stone, and yet be so soft that it could be wrapped around the body. He does not believe that it is the will by which a man should steady himself, yes, that when all fails, that it is the will that a man must hold to. He does not believe that the will is itself the mover, but rather that it should itself be mover, that in itself it is fluctuating and on that account should be supported, held firm, that it should be moved and supported by causes, considerations, advice of others, experiences, rules of life. If we, quite properly, should compare the will in man with the headway impetus of a ship in which he (the man) is carried forward: then he believes, on the contrary, that the will, instead of its propelling all, is itself something that should be tugged forward, that there are grounds, considerations, advice of others, experiences, rules of life, that go alongside of and push or pull the will forward as if the will could be compared to a barge—yes, to a freight barge. But in the same stroke the will is made impotent, "up to a certain degree" discounted in relation to causes, considerations and advice,

and in relation to how these react upon one another. He
has turned everything around. What for each one, who
with the impetus of eternity steers for a better world,
would be a hindrance in life, he takes for an advantage in
hastening forward, and what should be an advantage in
hastening forward, he makes into a delay, or at least into
something that is in itself neutral. Such a person must
certainly remain in double-mindedness, upon the inland
lake of double-mindedness, busy with trivialities, if, instead
of charting a course out of all this delaying by means of
the will to the Good, he only sails with the speed of the
hindrance.

A man enters upon his life, hoping that all will go well
for him and with good wishes for others. He steps out
into the world's multiplicity, like one that comes from the
country into the great noisy city, into the multiplicity
where men engrossed in affairs hurry past one another,
where each looks out for what belongs to him in the vast
"back and forth," where everything is in passing, where
it is as though at each instant one saw what he had learned
borne out in practice, and in the same instant saw it refuted, without any cessation in the unrest of work, in multiplicity—that all too vast a school of experience. For here
one can experience everything possible, or that everything
is possible, even what the inexperienced man would least
believe, that the Good sits highest at the dinner table and
crime next highest, or crime highest and the Good next
highest—in good company with each other. So this man
stands there. He has in himself a susceptibility for the
disease of double-mindedness. His feeling is purely immediate, his knowledge only strengthened through contemplation, his will not mature. Swiftly, alas, swiftly he is
infected—one more victim. This is nothing new, but an old
story. As it has happened to him, so it has happened with

the double-minded ones who have gone before him—this in passing he now gives as his own excuse, for he has received the consecration of excuses.

Perhaps at this point a speaker, who was just as double-minded as that double-minded one, and therefore really only wishes to deceive, will describe the willing of the Good for us in an alluring fashion, yet, in an alluring fashion with the prospect of becoming something in the world. Perhaps he will close his description by saying that that double-minded person came to nothing in the world—just to terrify us. But we do not wish to deceive. Still less do we wish to stir up terror, to frighten by a fraud, which is much like commending a falsehood. We wish only to say that, eternally understood, the double-minded one came to nothing. On the other hand, in the time order, in keeping with his ability and his indefatigable industry, he probably became a well-to-do man, a respected man—or to a certain degree, a respected man, or at least what a man can become within the circumference of "to a certain degree." And by this it is not denied, that he could readily become the richest man in the world. For that, too, the condition of being the richest man, is only something "to a certain degree." Only the determinations of eternity are above "a certain degree." Like its truths, the time order with all that belongs to it is to a "certain degree"; only eternity and its truth is eternal. Therefore let us not deceive and say that in an earthly sense a man advances furthest in the time order by willing the Good in truth. Do not let the talk be as double-minded as the world is. No, in the time order a man advances furthest, in an earthly sense, by means of double-mindedness, and, it must be admitted, mainly by that double-mindedness that has about it a spurious gloss of unity and of inner coherence.

Behold! Honesty is the most enduring of all. It endures,

too, at the time when the rich man becomes poor by his
honesty. It still endures when the once rich but later poor
man is dead and gone, and when the world has been de-
stroyed and forgotten, and when there is neither poverty
nor wealth nor money; or further still, when the once
rich, but later poor man has long since forgotten the suffering of poverty, yet his honesty still endures. And yet
suppose a man should believe that honesty is only related
to money and to money values, that the same thing happens
to it as to dishonesty, that it ends with the end of the
order of money values. Yes, to be sure, honesty stands related to wealth, and poverty and money, but it also stands
related to the Eternal. And it does not stand related in a
double-minded fashion to money and to the Eternal, so
as to aim at joining itself in a financial relationship—to
the Eternal. Because of this it endures. It does not "to a
certain degree" endure the longest of all. It endures. That
assertion is, therefore, no mere proverb. It is an eternal
truth. It is the invention of eternity.

On the other hand, there is a proverb that says: One
needs a little more than honesty to get through this world.
But the questions to which these assertions are a reply differ
most widely. It is asked, what is it that endures; and it is
asked, how may I pass through? He that merely asks, how
may I pass through, has no desire for real knowledge. But
he that asks what it is that endures has already passed
through; he has already gone over from the time order to
eternity, although he is still alive. The one inquires of
things only in comparatives. The other questions eternally and if in the hour of temptation, when his honesty is
tested, he asks properly, he will receive now, and in the
next world he will again receive eternity's answer: Yes, it
endures! Yes, it is better to go to the house of mourning
than to the house of feasting,[21] for there one can learn, that

after a hundred years, all is forgotten. Yes, to be sure, long
ago the feast and the gallant brothers were forgotten, but
truly the Eternal is not forgotten, not after a thousand
years.

8. The Price of Willing One Thing:
Commitment, Loyalty. Readiness to Suffer All

B. IF A MAN SHALL WILL THE GOOD IN TRUTH, THEN HE
MUST BE WILLING TO DO ALL FOR THE GOOD OR BE
WILLING TO SUFFER ALL FOR THE GOOD.

MY LISTENER, before going further, if it seems
right to you, we shall look at the course our talk has taken
up to this point. For the talk, too, has its laborious development, and it is only when this is completed in the necessary
slowness that we may come to an understanding with
each other about what the talk presupposes. Only at that
point can the talk, being then secure, make use of the agreeable speed that is properly the very life of conversation.
Thus, purity of heart is to will one thing, but *to will one
thing could not mean to will the world's pleasure and what
belongs to it*, even if a person only named one thing as his
choice, *since this one thing was one only by a deception.
Nor could willing one thing mean willing it in the vain
sense of mere bigness* which only to a man in a state of giddiness appears to be one. FOR IN TRUTH TO WILL ONE THING,
A MAN MUST WILL THE GOOD. This was the first, *the possibility of being able to will one thing*. But in order GEN-

UINELY TO WILL ONE THING, A MAN MUST IN TRUTH WILL THE GOOD. On the other hand, as for each act of willing the Good which does not will it in truth, it must be declared to be double-mindedness. Then there was a type of double-mindedness that in a more powerful and active sort of inner coherence seemed to will the Good, but deceptively willed something else. It willed the Good *for the sake of reward, out of fear of punishment, or as a form of self-assertion*. But there was another kind of double-mindedness *born of weakness*, that is commonest of all among men, that versatile double-mindedness that wills the Good in a kind of sincerity, but only wills it "to a certain degree."

Now the talk may continue. If, then, a man in truth wills the Good, then HE MUST BE WILLING TO DO ALL FOR IT or HE MUST BE WILLING TO SUFFER ALL FOR IT. Once more we understand that this classification divides mankind, or rather reminds us of a division that exists in reality: a division into the active ones and the sufferers, so that when the talk is about willing to do all, we may think about the suffering which this act may entail without calling such a man a sufferer, since he actually is an active person. But by the sufferers, we think of those to whom life itself seems to have assigned the speechless, and if you will, the useless sufferings, useless because the sufferings are not benefitting others, are helping nothing at all, but rather are a burden both to others and to the sufferers themselves.

I. *If a man shall will the good in truth, then he must be willing to do all for the Good.*

Let us first consider: the willingness to do all for the Good. All—yet will not this talk easily exceed all bounds, if all is named? Will it not become an impossibility to master all the differences included under the term "all," and as a result will the talk not become vague, since the Good can demand the most different things of different people? It can sometimes demand that a man leave his esteemed calling and put on lowliness, that he give away all his possessions to the poor, that he shall not even dare to bury his father.[22] Again it can demand of others that they shall assume the power and the dignity that are offered them, that they shall take over the working power of wealth, that they shall bury the father, and that perhaps a large part of their lives shall be consecrated to faithfulness which is to be faithful over the little to this extent, that their own life has no claims of its own, but rather is faithful to the memory of a departed one. Now let us not multiply confusion and distraction in a host of individual details. For these also remind us of the struggle of pettiness for preference, where one person thinks that by doing one thing he is doing more for the Good than another who does something else. For if both in relation to the demand do all, then they do equally much. And if neither of them does all, then they do equally little. Instead of multiplying details, let us simplify this all into its essential unity and likeness by saying that to will to do all is: *in the commitment to will to be and to remain loyal to the Good.* Because the commitment is just the committing of all, just as it is also that which is essentially one thing. In this way no tempting occasion for the mistaken quarrel of pettiness about preference need arise. Then, too, the talk can be briefer, for it is unnecessary to enumerate variety's many names and yet be in keeping with strict accuracy, since this essential brevity answers to that rich brevity which is present in life, in the act of commitment to will to be and to remain loyal to the Good. No one believes that this is a long-drawn-out affair. On the contrary, from the standpoint of eternity, if I dare say so, it is this abbreviating of all

of life's fractions (for eternity's length is the true abbre-
viation) that frees life of all its difficulties, and it is
through deciding to will to be and to remain loyal to the
Good that so much time is gained. For that which absorbs
men's time when they complain about the lack of time is
irresoluteness, distraction, half thoughts, half resolutions,
indecisiveness, great moments—great moments. It was because of these that we said: to be and to remain loyal to,
so that the commitment should not be confused with the
extravagance of an expansive moment. The person, who
in decisiveness wills to be and to remain loyal to the Good,
can find time for all possible things. No, he cannot do
that. But neither does he need to do that, for he wills only
one thing, and just on that account he will not have to do
all possible things, and so he finds ample time for the
Good.

The commitment of willing to be and to remain loyal
to the Good is truth's brief way of expressing: to be willing to do all. And in this expression there is apparent that
leveling insight that recognizes no distinction proportionate
to that actual difference of life or of human circumstances:
to be an active person or to be a sufferer, because the
sufferer too, can be committed to the Good. This is of
importance to the thought and to the talk, so that discord
shall neither exist nor be kindled; so that the talk shall
not incite the active person who is able to accomplish much
in the outer world to compare himself in a conceited way
with the sufferer; nor provoke the heavily laden sufferer
who apparently spends his time in useless suffering, de-
spairingly to compare his uselessness, his pain, his not
merely superfluous, but for others even burdensome existence, with the great accomplishments of the active ones.
Alas, often enough such an unfortunate person, in addition
to his heavy, innocent suffering must bear the severe judg-

ment of the arrogant, the busy, and the stupid, who are indeed able to irritate and hurt him, but who can never understand him.

So now let us talk of doing all, and speak of the men who, in this or that way, are assigned to the external world as to a stage. It makes no difference at all, God be praised, how great or how small the task may be. In relation to the highest of all this simply does not matter when it comes to being willing to do all. Oh, how great is the mercy of the Eternal toward us! All the ruinous quarreling and comparison which swells up and injures, which sighs and envies, the Eternal does not recognize. Its claim rests equally on each, the greatest who has ever lived, and the most insignificant. Yes, the sun's rays do not shine with more equality on the peasant's hut and the ruler's palace, than the equality with which the Eternal looks down upon the highest and the lowest. Yet not equally, for if the most exalted is not willing to do all, then eternity gazes in wrath upon him. And, even though the rich man by human ingenuity should at last succeed in being able to trick the sun into shining more invitingly upon his palace than over the poor man's hut, man will never be able to trick the Good and eternity in this fashion. The demand upon each is exactly the same: to be willing to do all. If this be fulfilled then the Good bestows its blessing equally upon each one who makes and remains loyal to his commitment.

Suppose that we should now in earthly and temporal fashion recommend the commitment. Suppose we should say, "It does not matter whether you leap into it or creep into it. You may as well risk it first as last. For although you may very well succeed for a time in dancing on roses, nevertheless the difficult time of trouble will come, and so it is always well to be prepared." Oh, let us never wish to sell what is holy, or more properly, let us never forget that in this sense eternity is not for sale, that it regards itself as too good to be sold where it might be bought by a bargainer—a brazen one. Yes, for the same reason that a temple-robber is the most contemptible of criminals, so it is with this highly painted clever one who cunningly wills the highest thing of all without willing it in truth. The temple-robber may even succeed in plundering the sacred treasures, and may actually get them into his possession since these treasures are something external. But that clever one never succeeds in stealing the commitment or in stealing himself into the commitment. The ever-active righteousness that eternally dispenses justice is so vigilant that every criminal not only does not become dangerous to the Eternal, but in the sense of imperfection does not even actually come into existence, since it becomes a self-accusation. In relation to the Eternal, the criminal's worst act is much as if the temple-robber instead of stealing the sacred vessels went to the high temple officials and said, "I wish to steal the sacred vessels." So with the matter of stealing the commitment, it does not succeed, but instead the guilty one announces himself to the Eternal and says, "I wish to steal the commitment." For in eternity there is no sensory illusion, and so neither is there what in a moral sense is the same thing, any actual possession— of stolen goods. Let us not, then, deceptively and uselessly recommend the coming to a decision. If someone wishes to sneak through life, let him do it. The truth might still take occasion to seize him so that he would will the decision for the sake of the Good. But let us not make him believe that by an artifice he could cunningly carry the commitment with him on his stealthy way through life.

The decision is, to be willing to do all for the Good; it is not cleverly to wish to have the advantage of the Good. Alas, there is in every man a power, a dangerous and at the same time a great power. This power is cleverness. Cleverness strives continually against the commitment. It fights for its life and its honor, for if the decision wins, then cleverness is as if put to death—degraded, to become a despised servant whose talk is attentively listened to, but whose advice one does not stoop to follow.

Now in the inner world man uses cleverness in a ruinous way, in order to keep himself from coming to a decision. In countless ways cleverness can be so misused; but in order once again not to multiply that which is not important and thereby to divert attention from the really important, we will again simply designate this misuse by a definite expression: to seek to evade. To forsake one's post, to desert in battle is always disgraceful, but cleverness has invented an ingenious device that apparently prevents flight: it is evasion. By the help of evasion, namely, one does not come into danger, and neither does he lose his honor by running away in danger—on the contrary one does not come into danger—that is one advantage. And one wins great honor as being especially clever—that is a second advantage. Only eternity, the Good, and so also the Holy Scriptures, are of another opinion about this matter of evasions and about the much-honored clever ones. For they are referred to when it speaks of, "those that draw back into perdition" (Hebrews 10:39). How strange that a man can, therefore, avoid a danger, and when he believes himself secure and saved (which one indeed should believe after he has escaped danger), just at that point he has sunk into perdition.

A clever one speaks in this way, "Afterwards it is too late. If I have already ventured too far out and been crushed, who will help me then? Then I should be a cripple for all the rest of my life, an object of mockery and a byword among men. Who will help me then?" Who will

help him then? Who other than the power in which he
trusted in venturing so far out? Yet surely not as one who
is stronger helps a weakling, but rather as when the unprofitable servant[23] does everything in order to do his lord's
will. But now with the help of evasions the clever one
talks as if the Good itself was no power, or as if its power
counted for nothing, so therefore, that it could be the
clever one, who (if he chose to risk it) by doing all, would
help out the Good. If this is so, then it is true enough that
no one exists who can help him—in case he actually should
venture out—and that which a clever ingenious imagination invents in order to be able to forget the troublesome
background of evasion above the terrifying foreground,
actually comes to pass. Evasion thus accomplishes nothing.

And even if the terrible thing now happens: the confident venturer is injured. Even an earthly government is
accustomed to care for its faithful servants who risk danger
in loyalty to the state, then shall not God and the Good
also care for their faithful servants, if only they are sincere!

And even if the terrible thing happens that when the
sincere person had risked all, that it was then that the government said to him, "My friend, I cannot use you." Oh,
how clear it is that the smallest crumb of grace in the
service of the Good is infinitely more blessed than to be
the mightiest of all outside that service. Verily, verily, it
is indeed true, it is with trembling true, in relation to the
ungodly, but it is also by grace happily true for the sincere, that God is not tricked by a man? Even if the sincere
one comes to grief, perhaps it was just this that the government needed. Has it not often happened that the well is
first covered only after the child has fallen in, while before
this the most reasonable arguments and warnings had been

of no avail? Now if the sincere one is willing to be the child who falls in, has his venture been wholly in vain?

Another says, "I have not the strength to risk all." Again evasion, an evasion by the aid of the word "all." For the Good is quite capable of reckoning and computing its demand in relation to the strength that this man has. And what is more, if he will venture in all sincerity, then he will certainly receive strength enough in the act of decision. But the clever one desires by the help of evasions to have strength in advance. He wishes to misuse it like the soldier who, in order to be sure of being distinguished in battle, demands his distinction in advance. And yet this picture is untrue, for it is doubtful how far the battle gives strength. But it is certain, that the confidence, wherewith he has ventured, does give superhuman strength. Yet it is also certain (oh, wonderful accuracy!) that the one who does not have trust does not receive this strength. Look, the great battleship first gets its orders when it is far out at sea, the little sloop knows all in advance. And in a spiritual sense, a person is only really out at sea who is willing to do all, irrespective of whether he is the highest or the least. The little sloop is the clever person, no matter whether he be the highest or the least.

One says, "The bit that I can do is not worth while." The clever one is polite, he understates, he says, "Do excuse me." He acts as if the Good were a distinguished man, and as if willing the Good were a distinguished act. But it is a misconception. No, here it is an evasion. The Good is not distinguished. It demands neither more nor less than all, whether that is a mere bit or not is neither here nor there. The widow's mite was all that she owned. Before God it was as great a sum as all of the world's gold in a single heap, and if one who owned all the gold in the world gave it all, he would give no more. Yes, when that public col

lection of money was made, it was possible that the collec-
tors both kindly and politely might have said to the widow,
"No, Mother, you keep your mite." But the Good—how
shall we express it? Its goodness is so great, that it recognizes no difference.

One man says, "I am not justified in doing that because
of my wife and children." Alas, even the civil government
looks after, yes . . . yet this is out of place here. But I
wonder if he, as man and father, really could do anything
better for wife and children than to impress upon them
this trust in Providence. Here, then, it is not as in civil
life that the person who risks dares hope that the state
will look after his wife and children. No, spiritually understood, he has by his venture cared for them in the best
possible way, for by this he has shown them that he at
least has faith in Providence. Here, then, it is not as in
civil life that the person who undertakes to risk can do it
by caring for wife and children. For spiritually understood, the fearful one shows that he has no concern for
the true welfare of wife and children.

One may say, "Experience teaches that it is best to divide
one's energies in order that one can win by the one, when
he loses by another. I owe it to myself, and to my future,
not to place all upon a single thing." Yes, God grant that
he will not restrict his pains to his future, for that is too
little; but may this alone be set before his eyes, and ever
called to his mind; that his future is—an eternity.

Yet how could one ever finish talking about all the evasions? Who would undertake this fruitless work, this battle
with the air! And even if someone should, even if he succeeded in enumerating them all and for an instant succeeded in holding them together so that they could not,
like true runaways, slip away and assume another role
while remaining in essence the same, still one evasion would

always remain behind even if none ought to be there, even
if by repeated inspection a commendable cleverness should
be unable to discover that a single ground had been overlooked and hence that a single evasion was still possible.

So the double-minded person, seduced by cleverness,
yielded to the evasions. "But this brought him nothing."
Oh, let us not deceive youth, let us not sit and bargain
in the outer court of the holy, nor formulate a profane
introduction to the holy, as if one should in truth will the
Good in order to prosper in the world. Readily grant that
the clever one amounts to something, even to something
great in the world. There is, however, a power that is called
memory. It should be dear to all the good ones as well as
to all lovers. Yes, it may even be so dear to lovers that they
almost prefer this whisper of memory to the sight of each
other, as when they say, "Do you remember that time, and
do you remember that time?"

Now memory also visits the double-minded person. Then
it says to him, "Do you remember that time? . . . You
as well as I knew well enough what was there required
of you, but you shrank back (to your own destruction),
do you remember that! It was by this that you won a
great deal of your property (to your own destruction). Do
you remember that! Do you recall that time? . . . You
knew as well as I what you should venture, you knew
what danger it involved, do you remember, you shrank
back (to your own destruction), do you remember? . . .
Yet it served you well, for the badge of honor on your
breast calls you back to a memory of how you shrank back
to your own destruction!

"Do you remember that time . . . you knew well
enough by yourself and by my solitary voice in your heart,
what you should choose, but you shrank back (to your
own destruction), do you remember that? It was that time

when the popular favor and the exultation of the masses
hailed you as the righteous one, do you remember that?"
Yes, it indeed becomes your concern to remember the
popular exultation and favor, for in eternity such things
are not recognized. But in eternity it is not forgotten that
you shrank back! For what shall it profit a man if he
shall gain the whole world and lose his own soul.[24] What
shall it profit him, if he shall gain the time order and all
it possesses, if he breaks with the Eternal? What shall it
profit him if he comes through the world under full sail
aided by the favorable winds of popular exultation and
admiration, if he runs aground upon eternity? What shall
it profit the sick man to imagine himself, as all men do,
to be well, if the physician says he is sick!

Outwardly, too, cleverness is used in a ruinous way, in
the matter of the decision, that is to say, it is outwardly
misused. And we are indeed speaking of the active ones,
and of being willing to do all for the Good. Here cleverness may be misused in a multitude of ways. But, once
more, let us not increase the distracting element. Let us,
rather, simplify that which is significant, and call all these
different kinds of misuse by a single name: deception. The
clever one knows just how the Good must be altered a tiny
particle in order to win the world's good will. He knows
how much should be added to it and how much should
be subtracted. He knows just what ingratiating thing
should be whispered in men's ears, what should be entrusted
to their hands, and how the hand should be pressed, how
it should be swung away from truth's decision, how the
turning should be done, and how he himself in suppleness
should shift and turn—"in order that he can accomplish
all the more for the Good." But the secret of deception, to
which in one way or another all the expressions can be
traced back, is this: that certainly it is not men that stand

in need of the Good, but that it is the Good that stands
in need of men. On that account it is men who must be
won. For the Good is a poor beggar that is in desperate
need, instead of its being men who are in need of the
Good, and so much in need of it that it is the one thing
necessary to them, that it must be bought at any price,
that absolutely all must be given up and sold in order to
buy it, but that also, the one who owns it owns all. Yet
it happens that all are naturally fooled by the deception.
Someone makes an attempt to fool the Good, which in all
eternity inevitably fails, for that it seems to succeed for
a fortnight or a lifetime is only a jest. The clever one, on
the other hand, wins great distinction in the world—and
he, too, is fooled. The crowd delights itself with the flattering sweets of imagination—and is fooled! This was deception's secret, that it is the Good that stands in need of
men. The clever one's secret is, that he cannot be wholly
content with the Good's poor reward, but must cast about
to earn a little extra by eluding the Good a little.

Seduced by cleverness, the double-minded person yielded,
"but he accomplished nothing in this world." No, let us
not give a false impression; he accomplished much. A large
number of friends of the Good, or of good friends rallied
admiringly around him. Of course, they believed by this
to attach themselves once more to the Good, but that certainly must be a deception, for the clever one himself went
outside the Good. Many joined together, for they had the
idea that the Good is something extraordinary, and all
honor be to them and all honor be to this true idea. But
they also had the idea that the Good is something so ex-
ceptionally great that many must join together in order to
buy it. Yet this conception is not worthy of honor, even
if it be deceptively called humility. It is an insult to the
Good, which in its infinite goodness does not refuse the

most insignificant, but allows him also to bid and to buy—
if he is willing to do all and so in truth to honor the Good.
On the other hand, the Good rejects all stupid honor and
distinction, where its greatness would be compared with an
estate which the "individual" has not money enough to
buy so that it is necessary to take up a collection. With
the help of the masses the clever one now erected an
enormous building. True enough, it was only a frame building (there were many others like it), but it looked well as
long as it stood. But memory, memory that in the highest
and most sober sense purifies even the coarser expressions
is what in plain everyday language is called a "dun-
ner." Now and then memory even pays a visit to the popular idol. Upon these occasions, memory murmurs softly
to him, "Can you remember the deceptive turn you gave
the thing, by which you won the blind masses, and by
which you were able to build the tower so high?" But the
popular one says, "Only keep quiet, never let anyone get
to know it." "Very well," memory answers. "You know
that I am no petty bickerer who is in desperation over
what is owed him. Let it rest. No one shall get to know
it, as long as you live, perhaps not even when you are dead
and forgotten. But eternally, eternally it will continue to
be remembered." Oh, what did it net the unprofitable
servant, if his Master went away, if his Master traveled so
far away that he should never more see him in this life,
what good was this to him, if the Master that traveled away
was memory with which he must be together throughout
eternity! What help is it indeed to the condemned one, if
the day of punishment is put off throughout his whole life;
how does this help him, if indeed the judgment that was
passed on him is the judgment of eternity and shall be carried out in eternity!

The clever one, therefore, accomplishes much. Let us for

once think through this thought: *to accomplish something
in the world.* One hears so much of both impatient and
misleading talk about this. To be sure, it is well that all
should wish to do something. It is indeed earnestness to
desire it, but should it not also be earnestness to understand
in oneself and in life precisely what is meant by saying
that one man accomplishes such an exceptional amount, or
that another man seems to accomplish nothing at all. Suppose the temporal order is not understood as it pictures itself, but rather as the recognizable fact that it is in reality.
Suppose the temporal order was a homogeneous transparent
medium of the Eternal. Then every eternal volition in a
man, and every volition of the Eternal would straightway
become perceptible in the temporal order, if the same kind
of powers of comprehension be assumed in the temporal
order: so that when the man who wills does get on in the
temporal order, and is accounted to be something in the
eyes of the many, the eternal volition in a man would be
plainly evident, just as the quantity of a cry is obvious by
the quantity of the sound in a room, just as when a stone
is cast into the water its size is evident by the size of the
circle it makes. If matters stood like this between the temporal order and the Eternal, so that they answer each other
as the echo answers to the sound, then that which is accomplished would be a trustworthy rendering of the eternal
volition in a man. By what a man had accomplished, one
could immediately see how much will toward the Eternal
there was in him. But in that case it could never have
come to pass in the temporal order (in order to mention
the highest and the most horrible, but also what is the key
that explains all) that God's son, as He was revealed in
human form, was crucified—repudiated by the temporal
order. For He truly willed the Eternal in the eternal sense,
and yet in the temporal order He became distinguished by

being repudiated, and so accomplishing but little. As it had happened to God's son, so it went with the Apostles, just as they themselves had expected, and so it has gone with so many witnesses of the Good and the true in whom this eternal will has burned fiercely.

It is obvious, then, that the temporal order cannot be the transparent medium of the Eternal. In its given reality the temporal order is in conflict with the Eternal. This makes the determination to accomplish something less plain. The more active the Eternal is toward the witness, the stronger is the cleavage. The more the striver, instead of willing the Eternal, is linked with temporal existence, the more he accomplishes in the sense of the temporal existence. So it is in many ways or in all possible ways in the temporal order. When a peculiar thinker, who just by his peculiarity is more tied up with the Eternal and less with time's moment, addresses his speech to men, he is rarely understood or listened to. When, on the other hand, a voluble follower comes to his aid in order that the peculiar one can become—misunderstood: then it succeeds, then there are many who instantly understand it. The thinker becomes a kind of superfluous element in life, the follower an effective man who accomplishes such an extraordinary amount in the temporal order. Only upon a rare occasion does it ever happen that the Eternal and the temporal's accomplishments conform after a fashion to each other—by accident. For let us not insult God and the God-Man by assuming that what happened to Him there was an accident, that His life expressed something accidental, perhaps something that had He lived at another time, among another people, would not have happened to Him. If, then, there is to be significance in the talk about accomplishing, a distinction must be made between the momentary and the eternal view of the thing. These are two

opposed views which each man has to choose between in
regard to his own striving and in regard to each contemporary striving. For to judge by the outcome (whereby
an attempt is made to unite a judgment of temporal existence and of eternity into a judgment that comes after the
event is past) is not humanly possible in the instant that
a man himself acts, nor is it possible in the instant when
others act.

By the help of a sense deception, a living generation
often believes itself able to pass judgment on a past generation, because it misunderstood the Good. And it is even
guilty of committing the same offense against a contemporary. And yet it is just in regard to his contemporary
that a man should know whether he has the view of the
moment, or the view of the Eternal. At some later date, it
is no art to decorate the graves of the noble and to say,
"If they had only lived now," now—just as we are starting in to do the same thing against a contemporary. For
the difficulty and the test of what dwells in the one who
judges is precisely—the contemporary. The view of the
moment is the opinion which in an earthly and busy sense
decides whether a man accomplishes anything or not. And
in this sense, nothing in the world has ever been so completely lost as was Christianity at the time that Christ was
crucified. And in the understanding of the moment, never
in the world has anyone accomplished so little by the
sacrifice of a consecrated life as did Jesus Christ. And yet
in this same instant, eternally understood, He had accomplished all. For He did not foolishly judge by the result
that was not yet there, or more rightly (for here is the
conflict and battleground of the two interpretations of
what is meant by "accomplishing") the result was indeed
there. Question His contemporaries, if you ever meet them.
Do they not say of the crucified one, "The fool, he would

help others and he cannot help himself, but now the outcome also shows, so that everyone may see what he was."[25] Was it not said by His contemporaries, especially where the clever led the conversation, "The fool, he who had it in his power to become king if he cared to make use of his opportunity, if he had only half my cleverness, he would have been king. In the beginning I really believed that it was ingenuity, that he let these people express themselves in this fashion without wishing to give himself up to them. I believed it was a trick in order to inflame them still more. But now the result shows clearly enough what I more recently have myself been quite clear about, that he is a shallow, blind visionary!" Was it not said by many intelligent men and women, "The result shows that he has been hunting after phantasies; he should have married. In this way he would now have been a distinguished teacher in Israel."

And yet, eternally understood, the crucified one had in the same moment accomplished all! But the view of the moment and the view of eternity over the same matter have never stood in such atrocious opposition. It can never be repeated. This could happen only to Him. Yet eternally understood, He had in the same moment accomplished all, and on that account said, with eternity's wisdom, "It is finished."

For it is not after the passage of eighteen hundred years that He will now again appear, and referring to the outcome, say, "It is finished." In contrast to this, He would still not say that. Perhaps it would require many centuries before He would be able to say that in regard to temporal existence. Yet what He is still unable to say after the passage of eighteen triumphant centuries, He said in His own age, eighteen centuries ago, in the very moment when all was lost. Eternally understood, He said. "It is finished."

"It is finished." He said that just when the mass of the people, and the priests, and the Roman soldiers, Herod and Pilate, and the idle ones on the street, the crowd in the gateway, and the newspaper reporters (if there were any such at that time) in short, when all the powers of the moment, however different their sentiments might have been, were agreed upon this view of the matter: that all was lost, hopelessly lost. "It is finished," He said, nailed to the cross as He was, at the very time when His Mother stood there—as if nailed to the cross, when His disciples' eyes were as if nailed to the cross by horror at this sight. Hence Motherhood and faithfulness submitted to the moment's view of the matter, that all was lost. Oh, then let us by this most horrible thing, which once took place (and that it happened only once is not to the world's credit, but rather that the crucified one is eternally and essentially different from every other man) let us learn wisdom in the lesser relationships. Let us never deceive youth by foolish talk about the matter of accomplishing. Let us never make them busy in the service of the moment, instead of in patience willing something eternal. Let us not make them quick to judge what they perhaps do not understand, instead of willing something eternal and being content with little for themselves! Let us rightly consider that a generation is not on that account superior because it understands that a previous generation acted wrongly, if in the present moment they themselves do not understand how to discriminate between the momentary and the eternal aspect of the thing at hand.

9. The Price of Willing One Thing:
The Exposure of Evasions

But the one who in truth wills the Good, puts cleverness to an inward use: in order to prevent all evasions and thereby to help him enter into and persist in the commitment.

CLEVERNESS IS INDEED a great power, yet it is treated by him as an insignificant servant, as a shrewd contemptible one. He hears the servant, to be sure, but in action he is not guided by him. He uses cleverness against himself as a spy and informer, which informs him instantly of each evasion, yes, even gives warning at any suspicion of an evasion. Now just as the thief knows the hidden way—and goes by it, so the authorities also know it and go by it in order to detect the thief, but the knowledge as knowledge is the same in both cases.

This is the way he makes use of cleverness. I do not know whether it is true that at each man's birth two angels are born, his good and his bad angel. But this I do believe (and I will gladly listen to any objection, although I will not believe it) that at each man's birth there comes into being an eternal vocation for him, expressly for him. To be true to himself in relation to this eternal vocation is the highest thing a man can practice, and, as that most profound poet has said: "Self-love is not so vile a sin as self-neglecting."[26] Then there is but one fault, one offense: disloyalty to his own self or the denial of his own better self. One who is guilty of such a fault is not like a thief or a robber. The

civil authority will not lie in wait for him. This fault may
begin its course in complete silence so that none will be
aware of it. Is it, therefore, perhaps of no account? Certainly many believe that a man can search out and grasp
the Truth just as well, creatively express the Beautiful
just as well, vitally perfect the Good just as well, even if,
in order to win some advantage in the world, he was
secretly a little unfaithful to himself, even if he did shift
the boundary stones of his inner life a particle by just a
shade less scrupulousness, so that even though he had won
this material advantage by doubtful means, yet he "can
truly work for the Good, the Beautiful, and the True."
So low an estimate of the Good and the Beautiful and the
True is expressed by this as to think that it ought to be
able to make use of anyone as a serviceable instrument
from whom to elicit a harmonious strain, anyone—even
the one that had polluted himself!

Yes, man can deceive himself and men. But when eternity listens attentively, listens in order to discover whether
the playing of the strings is pure and in time with itself—
alas, it instantly detects false tones and hesitation. It rejects such a man just as a connoisseur rejects a stringed
instrument when it is damaged. Alas, it is indeed a sorry
cleverness (however much it boasts of the material advantage that it won as a proof—of its folly; however much
it points to the badges of distinction and thereby again
to—the hidden dejection within), a sorry cleverness that
deceives itself about what is the highest of all. The only
genuine cleverness is that which helps a man in all de-
votedness truly to will the Good.

The one who truly wills the Good, therefore, makes use
of cleverness against evasions. But by this does he not
achieve something great in the world? Perhaps so, perhaps
not. But one thing definitely he does become: he becomes

a friend, a lover of memory. And so when in a quiet hour, memory visits him (and already at this point how different it is from that visit when memory threateningly knocks at the door of the double-minded man!), then it says to him, "Do you remember that time, that time when the good resolution conquered within you?" And he answers, "Yes, dear one!" But then memory continues (and between lovers memory is so dear that they almost prefer to the sight of each other the whisper of memory when they say, "Can you remember that time?" and "Can you remember that time?"), memory continues, "Can you remember all the hardships and sufferings you endured for the sake of the resolution?" He answers, "No, dear one, I have forgotten that—let it remain forgotten! But when in the toils of life and struggle, when in my troubled thoughts all is in confusion, it may seem to me as if even that was forgotten which I know I had willed in sincerity. Oh, thou hast thy very name from that act of remembering, thou messenger of the Eternal: Memory. At that hour, visit me, and bring with thee the long-desired, the strengthening meeting with thyself once more." And memory answers in parting, "I promise you that, I swear it to you by all eternity." Then they part one from another, for so it must be here in the world of time. Deeply moved, he takes one more look after memory's vanishing form as one looks after a glorified saint. Now it has gone and so has the quiet hour. It was only a quiet hour, it was not some great moment—on that account he hoped that memory would keep its promise. He preserved in his own soul that stillness in which he met with memory when it was pleased to visit him. To him this is his reward, and to him this reward is above all others. Yes, just as a Mother, who carries her beloved child asleep at her breast along a difficult road, is not troubled about what may happen to her, but only fears that the child may be disturbed and upset, so he, too, does not fear the troubles of the world on his own account. He is only troubled lest these should upset and disturb that possibility of a visit that slumbers in his soul.

The one who in truth wills the Good also uses cleverness on the outer world. It is no disgrace to be clever; it is a good thing. It is no disgrace that the authorities are clever, that they shrewdly know how to trace the criminal's hidden trail in order to seize him and make him harmless. In so far as the good man is clever, he, too, knows, how in the very face of truth the world wishes to have the Good made agreeable, how the crowd desires to be won—the much feared crowd, who "desire that the teacher shall tremble before his hearers and flatter them." He knows all about this—in order not to follow it, but rather by the very opposite conduct to keep as free as possible of these deceptions, that he himself may not adopt any illicit way of deriving some advantage from the Good (earning money, distinction, and admiration) and so that he may deceive no one by a figment of the imagination. Whenever possible he will prefer to withdraw the Good from contact with the crowd. He will seek to split the crowd up in order to get hold of the individual or to get each by himself. He will be reminded of what that simple old sage remarked in ancient times, "When they meet together, and the world sets down at an assembly, or in a court of law, or a theater, or a camp, or in any other popular resort, and there is a great uproar and they praise some things which are being said or done, and blame other things, equally exaggerating both, shouting and clapping their hands, and the echo of the rocks and the place in which they are assembled redoubles the sound of the praise or blame—at such a time will not a young man's heart, as they say, leap within him?"[27] And indeed this is exactly what is necessary in order in truth to will the Good—that a man's heart should leap, but leap with the unspoiled quality of youth. And therefore the good man, in case he is also a clever one, will see that if anything is able to be done for the Good, then he must try to get men to be alone. The same persons, who singly, as solitary individuals are able to will the Good, are immediately seduced as soon as they associate themselves and become a crowd. On that account the good man will neither seek to secure the assistance of a crowd in order to split up the crowd, nor will he seek to have a crowd back of him, during the time that he breaks up the crowd in front of him.

But just how the good man will make use of cleverness in the outer world does not permit of being more precisely specified in general terms, for that which is necessary can be totally different with respect to each time and to the circumstances of each time. That stern prophet[28] who went out into the desert and lived on locusts knew how, in relation to his contemporaries, he ought to express this decisively: that it is not the truth that is in need of men, but men who are in need of the truth. Hence they must come to him, come out into the desert. Out there, there was no opportunity for them to be able to decorate the truth, to be able most graciously to do something for it; out there where the ax did not lie in the woods, but at the foot of the solitary tree, and where each tree that did not bear good fruit was bound to be chopped down. Yes, to be sure, there have been self-appointed judges since that time, who have erred and chopped away at the whole forest—and the crowd found it most flattering. Again, there was that simple wise man, who worked for the Good under the form of a joke. He knew by his cleverness exactly what his frivolous people needed, in order that they should not simply take the earnestness of the Good in vain, and thereby

be led to pay the wise man a good deal of money as a reward for having deceived them. The form of the joke
prevented their misusing the Good's earnestness; the opposition of the joke, on the other hand, made their frivolity
obvious: it was the judgment.

Without this cleverness, the frivolous ones would in all
probability have imitated him in being earnest. Now, on
the contrary, he confronted them with the choice, and see,
they chose the joke. They never even noticed, that there
was anything earnest in it—because there was no earnestness in them. This was the judgment, and the judge's conduct. His art was paganism's highest ingenuity, for the
Christian type has still another consideration.

Yet this, too, may not be generalized upon. It applies
only to that initiated one, whose secret it is, so that by
paying close attention to such an individual, one can learn
to know a whole generation, concluding from him, from
the form he found it necessary to clothe himself in, how
the entire age must have been. But it is certain and
acknowledged by all, that each one who in truth wills the
Good, is not in the world in order to conjure up an appearance of the Good, thus winning approval in the eyes of
the world and becoming a man who is beloved by all. He
has not the task of changing the Good into a thing of the
moment, into something that shall be voted upon in a
noisy gathering, or something that swiftly gains some disciples who also will the Good up to a certain degree. No,
he has always the task, not by word, nor by intention, but
by the sincere inner concentration of his own life—the
task of making it most obvious of all that his surroundings have been set in opposition to him, not in order that
he shall judge in terms of words, but in order that his
life may unconditionally serve the Good in action. The
task is his own obligation in the service of the Good. Judg-

ing is not his real function, not his act, but is an accompaniment whereby the surrounding world relates itself to him. Judging is not his activity, because to will the Good in truth is his activity. Yet his suffering is an act of judging, because the surrounding world becomes manifest by the manner in which it lets him suffer; and at the same time by these sufferings he is helped to test himself as to whether it actually is the Good that he wills or whether he himself is caught up in a deception.

Above all, the one, who in truth wills the Good must not be "busy." In quiet patience he must leave it to the Good itself, what reward he shall have, and what he shall accomplish. He dare not allow himself a single word of compromise, not a glance. He dare not ask the slightest relief from the world. He has only to give himself up to the Good and to that thing and to that person that might possibly be helped by him. He is no judge. On the contrary, he is just the opposite, he is the one who is judged. He effects a judgment only in the sense that the surrounding world becomes manifest by how it judges him.

But in this way does he accomplish nothing at all, since he is weighed down with men's opposition, and then gets the worst of the battle? Now in this life indeed no, and in eternity, never. In this life indeed no, for the one who sincerely trusts in God is enthusiastic. He is not like a candle-stub, whose tiny flame goes out before a wind. No, he is like a great fire; a storm cannot quench it! And the flame in his fire is like that one in Greece: water cannot put it out! And even if finally the world does make him suffer, on that account neither the Good nor he has lost —for to be too far up in the world is most often, as in the ordeal that is called "trial by water," a sign of guilt. To be sure, since the world puts more store by the fashionable than by the truly Good, just on that account in the reckoning of the moment, he will accomplish far less by not giving in, not bargaining, not even making himself comfortable and powerful, by not willing to have profit for himself. But the remembering, the remembering! Let us indeed never forget the remembering, although a person might certainly believe that he would at least be able to forget. And shall not memory be able to remind him of that time when he sneaked away by underhanded means, in order to avoid a decision; of that time when he gave the matter another turn, in order to please men; of that time that he deserted his post, in order to let the storm pass over; of that time he knuckled under, in order to secure an easing off of his painful position; of that time he sought refuge and association with others—perhaps, as it is called, in order to work all the more effectively for the Good's victory, that is, in order to make his own position a little less difficult than as though at the midnight hour, somewhat terror-stricken, one stood all alone "with heavily loaded weapons at his dangerous post."[29]

Nay, what he accomplishes, and what he does not accomplish, in the sense of the moment, that is not his concern. He always accomplishes this—that he becomes the friend and lover of memory. He accomplishes this whether he is remembered in the world or not. For this world's memory is like the moment: a series of moments. Eternity's memory, that he is certain of. When he leaves this world, he leaves nothing behind him, he takes all with him, he loses nothing, he gains all—for "God is all to him."

10. The Price of Willing One Thing:

An Examination of the Extreme Case of an Incurable Sufferer

2. *If a man in truth wills the Good then he must be willing to suffer all for the Good.*

THIS APPLIES to the active ones. But from the sufferer, if he shall in truth will the Good, it is demanded that he must be willing to suffer all for the Good, or, as was previously explained, for the expression is essentially the same (and therein lies precisely the equal participation of the Eternal in the differentiations of earthly life), *he must be willing in his decision to be and to remain with the Good*. For he may also suffer and suffer and continue to suffer without ever arriving at any decision, in the true sense, of assenting to the suffering. A man may have suffered throughout his whole life without it ever, in any true sense, being able to be said of him that he has been willing to suffer all for the Good. But in that respect the sufferer's suffering is different from the active person's suffering, for when the active one suffers, then his suffering has significance for the victory of the Good in the world. When the sufferer, on the other hand, willingly takes up his appointed sufferings, he is willing to suffer all for the Good, that is, in order that the Good may be victorious in him.

Therefore, the sufferer must be willing to suffer all. All; but now how at this point shall the talk be conducted? For alas, even now the sight and the knowledge of suf-

fering can easily rob anyone of composure. How shall the
talk be briefly formulated? For the sufferings are able to
be so different, and of such long duration. Here, once
again, let us not multiply distractions but rather let us
simplify that which is really important. Let us center all
the talk about suffering upon *the wish*. For the wish is
the sufferer's connection with a happier temporal existence
(faith and hope are related to the Eternal through the
will) ; and at the same time the wish is the sore spot where
the suffering pains, the sore spot which the suffering continually touches. Even if suffering could still be spoken
of where there is no longer any wish, it is an animal-like
suffering, not suffering that befits a man. It is a kind of
spiritual suicide to will to put the wish to death. For we
are not talking about wishes, but rather about *the wish*
with the real emphasis of distinction, just as we also are
not talking about passing sufferings, but of the real sufferer. The wish is not the cure. This happens only by the
action of the Eternal. The wish is, on the contrary, the
life in suffering, the health in suffering. It is the perseverance in suffering, for it is as one thinker has said, "The
comfort of temporal existence is a precarious affair. It lets
the wound grow together, although it is not yet healed,
and yet the physician knows that the cure depends upon
keeping the wound open." In the wish, the wound is kept
open, in order that the Eternal may heal it. If the wound
grows together, the wish is wiped out and then eternity
cannot heal, then temporal existence has in truth bungled
the illness.

And so let us speak of the wish and thereby of the sufferings; *let us properly linger over this, convinced that
one may learn more profoundly and more reliably what
the highest is by considering suffering than by observing
achievements, where so much that is distracting is present.*

There are wishes that die in being born; there are wishes that are forgotten like our yesterdays; there are wishes that one outgrows, and later can scarcely recall; there are wishes that one learns to give up, and how good it was to have given them up; there are wishes from which one dies away, which one hides away, just as a departed one is hidden away in glorified memory. Those are the wishes to which an active person is exposed. They may be more or less dangerous diseases. Their cure may be accomplished by the extinction of the individual wish.

Yet there is also a wish that dies slowly, a wish that remains with the real sufferer even in the pain of his loss, and that only dies when he dies. For wishes concern particular objects, and a great number of objects, but the wish applies essentially to the whole life.

Yet sad as it is with the wish, how joyful it is with hope! For there is a hope that is born and dies; a short-lived hope, that tomorrow is forgotten; a childish hope, that old age does not recognize; a hope that one dies away from. But then—in death, in death's decision, a hope is born, that does not die in being born because it is born in death. By this hope the sufferer, under the pain of the wish, is committed to the Good. So it is with the hope in which the sufferer, as though from afar off, reaches out toward the Eternal.

With faith it is still more joyful. For there is a faith that disappoints and vanishes; a faith that is lost and is repented of; there is a faith, which, when it droops is like death. But then—in death, in death's decision a faith is won that does not disappoint, that is not repented of, that does not die; it seizes the Eternal and holds fast to it. By this faith, under the pain of the wish, the sufferer is committed to the Good. So it is with faith in which the sufferer draws the Eternal nearer to himself.

But with love it is most joyous of all. For there is a love, that blazes up and is forgotten; there is a love that unites and divides—a love *until* death. But then—in death, in death's decision, there is born a love that does not flame up, that is not equivocal, that is not—*until* death, but beyond death, a love that endures. In this love under the pain of the wish, the sufferer is committed to the Good. Oh, you sufferer, whoever you may be, will you then with doubleness of mind seek the relief that temporal existence can give, the relief that permits you to forget your suffering (yes, so you think) but rather that allows you to forget the Eternal! Will you in doubleness of mind despair, because all is lost (yes, so you think) yet with the Eternal all is to be won! Will you in doubleness of mind despair? Have you considered what it is to despair? Alas, it is to deny that God is love! Think that over properly, one who despairs abandons himself (yes, so you think); nay, he abandons God! Oh, weary not your soul with that which is passing and with momentary relief. Grieve not your spirit with forms of comfort which this world affords. Do not in suicidal fashion murder the wish; but rather win the highest by hope, by faith, by love—as the mightiest of all are able to do: commit yourself to the Good!

Once again let us speak of the wish, and hence of sufferings. A discussion of sufferings may always be profitable if it does not confine itself to the stubbornness of the affliction but is concerned whenever possible with the edification of the sufferer. It is both permissible and an act of sympathy to dwell upon suffering in order that the sufferer may not become impatient with our superficial discussion in which he does not recognize his own suffering and in order that in such impatience he may not thrust aside all consolation and be strengthened in double-

mindedness. It is indeed one thing to move out into life
with the wish when that which is wished for, continued
to be work and a task. It is another thing to move out
into life away from that wish. Look at Abraham.[30] He
had to leave the home of his fathers and journey out
among a strange people, where there was no reminder of
that which he loved—yes, it is true that sometimes it may
be a consolation, that nothing reminds one of what he
wishes to forget, but it is a bitter consolation for one who
is filled with longing. Hence a man can also have a wish
that for him contains all, so that in the hour of separation,
when the journeying is begun, it is as if he wandered out
into a strange land where nothing but the contrast with
what he has lost reminds him of that which he wished for.
It can be to him as if he journeyed into a strange land,
even if he remains in his home, perhaps on the same spot
—through the loss of the wish, indeed, it may be as if
he were among strangers, so that to suffer the loss of the
wish seems to him heavier and more critical than the loss
of his mind. Even if he does not leave the spot, his life
moves along a laborious path away from that wish, perhaps into useless sufferings, for we are talking of the real
sufferer, hence not of the ones who have the consolation
that their sufferings are serving some good cause, are of
benefit to others. It must have been like this: The journey
to the strange country was not long; in a moment he
was there, there in that strange country, where the sufferers were gathered, only not those that had stopped
grieving; not those whose tears eternity cannot wipe away,
for the reason that as an old religious writing so simply
and so touchingly says, "how shall God be able in heaven
to dry up your tears when you have not wept?"[31]

Another comes perhaps by another way but to the same
place. Silently, the guiding necessity leads him onward.

Austere and earnest, not cruel, for it is never cruel, duty
comes behind and brings up the rear of the company.
But the path is not the path of the wish. Now he halts
for a moment, even the two austere guides are touched
by his suffering: look, there a side path branches off;
"good-by, thou wish of my youth, thou friendly place,
where I had hoped to be able to build and to dwell with
my wish!" So they move on; the guiding necessity silently
in advance, duty austere and silent comes behind, not
cruel, for duty is never cruel. Alas, look, there a road
runs off to the side that leads to the wish; "good-by,
my place of work where by the full joy of work I had
hoped to be able to forget the wishes I was denied in
youth." So the company moved on. Yet the manner in
which it happens does not matter, whether it be the spot
that is altered and the sufferer remains at that same spot,
or whether the sufferer changes his whereabouts and jour-
neys away; this does not matter, if the place is the same,
if they are gathered at this one place, which human language may well be tempted to call: the useless suffering
that is beyond the reach of any comfort. The sufferings
themselves could have different names, but let us not
multiply names. Let us consider what is essential; that the
real sufferer does not benefit others by his suffering, but
rather is a burden upon them. If this latter is not the case,
the former must then be so if the suffering is to be regarded as useless, that is, if the sufferer is in the strictest
sense to be called a sufferer. In the strictest sense, and let
us really be strict with ourselves in order that we may
not venture to call ourselves sufferers, the first time anything goes against us; but let us be all the more tender
with those who are in the strictest sense sufferers. Oh,
such a sufferer, whoever you may be; if a man is come
to the point in the land of his birth where every way of

making a living is closed to him, then he thinks seriously
of emigrating to a foreign country and there seeking his
fortune. But perhaps you answer, "What does that mean,
how shall I be able to emigrate, and what good would
it do me to change my location? My lot is cast, everywhere
on earth it would be just the same." Of course, but let
us understand one another; the journey of which we speak
is not long, neither is the lot cast, unless you have already
found the way out of your suffering: it is only a single
step, a decisive step, and you, too, have emigrated, for the
Eternal lies much nearer to you than any foreign country
to the emigrant, and yet when you are there the change
is infinitely greater. So then, go with God to God, continually take that one step more, that single step that even
you, who cannot move a limb, are still able to take; that
single step, that even the prisoner, who has lost his freedom, even the one in chains, whose feet are not free, is
still able to take: and you are committed to the Good.
Nobody, not even the greatest that has ever lived, can do
more than you.

But bear in mind: your sufferings might well be called
useless, and that we men can certainly be tempted to speak
of useless suffering as beyond the reach of comfort. But
this is only human speech. In the language of eternity, the
suffering that helped you to reach the highest is far from
useless. Alas, it is only useless and unused when you will
not let yourself be helped by it up to the highest—for
perhaps you killed the wish and became spiritually like
dead flesh that feels no pain, otherwise it is just at the
point of the wish that the sufferer winces and that the
Eternal comforts.

Let us once again speak of the wish, and hence of sufferings. It is well not to turn away from the sight of
suffering too soon. *Let us properly dwell upon it, being*

convinced that for the deadly disease of "busyness" there is no medicine so specific as the pondering of the hard path of the true sufferer and as a fellow human being sharing with him in the common lot of suffering. But alas, how often man's sympathetic sharing in the suffering of others stands in inverse ratio to the length of the suffering! For if the suffering is drawn out in length, sympathy tends to pall: as the suffering increases, the sympathy decreases. At the first appearance of suffering, men's sympathy rushes out to the victim. But when the suffering lingers on, then sympathy subsides, and, on the part of the busy individual when the first active stage of his sympathy has waned, this sympathy at times changes into a certain bitterness against the sufferer. Yes: wishes could be healed after a time, they could become a part of the past: but not *the wish.* There is a real distinction here, for there is a pain of the wish which sympathy can fix upon, but there is also a pain of the wish that eludes all scrutiny, that conceals itself and secretly follows through an entire life. Yes, it follows, but in the sense of privation. Yes, like a faithful companion this pain follows the sufferer throughout his whole life and keeps him company, but there is no sympathy in attendance. Now in what way ought we to speak of this wish that may possibly exist but that withdraws into concealment, and yet speak so that the sufferer will acknowledge the description, so that he will not take offense and impatiently turn away from our officious account of sufferings which we are either not capable or have not had the time to think ourselves into? Let us then, wherever possible in the description, speak with the sufferer's own tongue and leave it to God to communicate to his heart any light that he may have for him.

Let us assume that dumb animals could have thoughts and could make themselves understood to one another even though we could not make out what they said, let us take that for granted. It seems almost as if this were so. For when in summer the peasant's horse stands in the meadow and throws up his head or shakes it, surely no one can know with certainty what that means; or when two of them who throughout their lives have walked side by side pulling in the same yoke are turned out at night, when they approach one another as if in intimacy, when they almost caress each other by movements of the head; or when the free horses neigh to one another so that the woods echo, when they are gathered on the plains in a big herd as if at a public meeting—assume then that they really could make themselves understood to one another.

But then there was one horse that was all alone. Now when this horse heard the call, when he saw that the herd was gathering in the evening, and he understood that they were about to hold a meeting, then he came running in the hope that he might learn something about life and its ways. He listened carefully to all that the elders had to say about how no horse should think himself fortunate until he is dead, how the horse of all creatures is most subject to the tragic changes of fate. And now the elder went over the many agonies: to suffer hunger and cold, to all but kill oneself through overwork, to be kicked by a cruel driver, to be abused by unskilled persons whom not a single step you take will satisfy, yet who blame and punish the horse for their own blunders, and then at last some winter, when old age has come on, to be driven out into the bare woods.

At this point the meeting broke up and that horse who had come with such eagerness went away dejected: "by sorrow of the heart the spirit is broken" (Proverbs 15:13). He had understood perfectly all that had been said, but no one there had even as much as mentioned his sufferings. Yet each time he noticed the other horses hurrying off to a gathering he came running eagerly, hoping always that now it would be spoken of. And each time he listened he went away with a heavy heart. He came to understand better and better what the others were concerned about, but he came to understand himself less and less, just because it seemed as though the others excluded him, although he, too, was present.

Oh, you sufferer, whoever you may be, if your suffering was not hidden because you wished to hide it (for then you can manage; *your* action calls for a different comment) but if it is because of misunderstandings then you, too, have gone among men, listened carefully to their explanations, sought out their instruction, taken part in their meeting. But each time you finished the book, and each time the conversation was over, and each time the "Amen" was pronounced: then was your spirit broken because your heart grew troubled as you sighed: "Oh, that such a thing was all that I suffered from!" Oh, but you are not wholly wanting in being understood, for even if you yourself may have done nothing to deserve it, you shall be bidden to the highest thing of all, and to the Most High Himself. Nor are you wholly without human sympathy. There is a common human concern that is called edification. It is not so common as those undertakings about which the crowd shouts and clamors, for each participant is in reality alone with himself, but yet in the highest and most inclusive sense, edification is a common human concern. The edifying contemplation finds no rest until it has come to understand you. Is not one sinner who repents more important to Heaven than ninety-nine righteous men[32] who have no need of repentance? So it is with you if you are one who truly suffers, your edifying contemplation is more important than the actions of

ninety-nine busy ones who have no need of edification.
Yes, even if you did not exist, the edifying contemplation
finds no rest before it has also plumbed this sorrow. For woe
to the edifying talk that wishes only to chat between man
and man about all the different inconveniences in life but
does not dare risk touching upon the more terrible sufferings: such a talk is without frankness and can but
have a bad conscience if it poses under the name of "edifying." The busy ones that neither toil nor are oppressed[33]
but are just busy, think that they have escaped when
they have contrived to avoid sufferings in this life; hence
they do not wish to be disturbed either by hearing or
thinking of that which is terrible. Yes, it is true that they
have escaped. They have also escaped having any insight
into life and have escaped into meaninglessness.

Oh, you sufferer, alone and abandoned as you are by
the generation to which you belong, know that you are
not abandoned by God, your creator. Everywhere you are
surrounded by His understanding which offers itself to you
at each moment. In it you unite your will with the Good.
And the edifying contemplation is always ready to remind
you of that presence; and its very existence is a source of
security to the living.

As it is a comfort to seafarers to know that no matter
on what strange water they may venture there are always
pilots within call, so the edifying contemplation stands
near the breakers and reefs of this life prepared by daily
sight of terrible sufferings swiftly to render what little
aid it can. Yet it cannot help in the way that a pilot helps
the ship. The sufferer must help himself. But then neither
shall he owe to this or to any other man what the seafarer
owes to the pilot. Indeed if this sufferer like anyone else
sincerely wills the Good, then he must be ready to suffer
all. Then he is committed, not in that commitment by

which he is exempted from suffering, but in that by which he remains intimately bound to God, in which he wills only one thing: namely, to suffer all, to be and to remain loyally committed to the Good—under the pain of the wish.

My listener! Perhaps you are tired of so much talk about suffering—but an edifying talk never tires of it, no, a mother may sooner tire of nursing her sick child than the edifying talk of speaking of suffering. You are perhaps what is called a "happy one" whom talk of this kind tires. Yet surely you are not so happy as to wish to remain coldly ignorant of sufferings; on the contrary you aspire to this knowledge of suffering for your own sake in order that your education may be improved by its somber spectacle! Or perhaps you are a sufferer, who is wearied by talking of so many different kinds of suffering when yours is not even mentioned. Oh, to edify oneself in a living way with the sufferings of others is a comfort, and to dwell too exclusively on one's own suffering may easily become that doubleness of mind which thinks that there is comfort for all others but none for itself. But this is not so. For with suffering each has his own, be it great or small. But with comfort it is certainly true that there is comfort for all, and in fact the same comfort for all.

Now let us once again speak of the wish, and hence of sufferings, for the duration of the suffering makes it heavier and heavier. But its duration depends as a matter of fact upon when the suffering began. A shrewd pagan has wisely observed that a man can accustom himself to protracted sufferings.[34] But the question here is, whether such comfort is the right thing. For what is being considered here is not how to find the readiest and best source of comfort, but rather how to will the Good in truth, how to will to suffer all in order to be and to remain committed to the Good.

Let us speak of a whole life of sufferings or of some person whom nature, from the very outset, as we humans are tempted to say, wronged, someone who from birth was singled out by useless suffering: a burden to others; almost a burden to himself; and yes, what is worse, to be almost a born objection to the goodness of Providence. Alas, the career of many a busy man is described by and gives rise to fresh *busyness*. The contemplation of such an unfortunate one is an excellent antidote for busyness. *For just by observing such a sufferer, one comes to know unmistakably what the highest is*. But we will not speak carelessly or in passing, hastening away from the sight of this suffering, absorbed in rejoicing over our having been spared it. Neither shall we speak despondently.

To be sure it is wonderful to be a child, to fall asleep upon the mother's breast only to awaken to see the mother again; to be a child and to know only the mother and the toy! We laud the happiness of childhood. The very sight of it soothes us by its smile, so that even the one to whom fortune is granted does not forget this down through the years. But, God be praised, it is not so ordered, that this should be the highest thing of all. It may be dispensed with without losing the highest thing of all. It may be absent without having lost the highest thing of all.

And to be sure it is fine to be young, to lie sleepless with the ferment of joyful thoughts, and to fall asleep only to wake up early with the song of the birds to continue the gaiety! We laud the happiness of youth. We rejoice with the joyful ones. We wish that youth might feel grateful for its happiness, and in the future we wish that it might be thankful for that which has vanished.

But, God be praised, it is not so ordered that this should be the highest thing of all. It may be dispensed with without losing the highest thing of all. It may be absent without having lost the highest thing of all.

And to be sure it is blessed to love, to be reduced to a single desire. What does it matter if all other desires are fulfilled or denied? There is but one desire, the loved one; one longing, the loved one; one possession, the loved one! We laud the happiness of love. Oh, that the fortunate one may be steadfast in the daily thankfulness of domestic life; that he may be faithful in the continuing thankfulness of remembrance. But, God be praised, it is not so ordered that this should be the highest thing of all. It may be dispensed with without losing the highest thing of all. It may be absent without having lost the highest thing of all.

But now the sufferer! Alas, there was no happy childhood for him. Of course a mother's love is faithful and tender, especially toward an ailing child. But a mother is also a human being. When he lay at his mother's breast, she did not gaze joyfully upon him. He saw that she was troubled. Sometimes when he wakened he noticed her weeping.

Even among grown-ups when they sit about depressed, let a man appear at the door, a happy, gifted one with light heart and gay spirit, and let him say, "Here am I!" and at once the merriment begins, and the clouds of care are routed. Such a gifted one is uncommon. But even the rarest genius of all, when can he bring in comparison to a child, when it makes its entrance amid the agonizing pain of the birth hour, opens the door and says, "Here am I!" Oh, the good fortune of childhood, to be so welcome!

Then he grew into a youth, but he never played with

the others, and if someone asked him, "Why do you not play with the others?" he might well have replied, "How have you the heart to ask me such a question?" So he withdrew from life, yet not with the object of dying, for he was still only a youth.

Then came the season of love, but no one loved him. Of course there were a few that were friendly toward him, but it was out of compassion and sympathy. Then he became a man, but he stood apart from life. Then he died, but even here he was not spared. For the little band that made up the mourner's train all said it was a blessing that God took him away, and the priest said the same thing. Then he was dead, and then he was forgotten— together with all of his useless sufferings. When he was born there was no gladness or rejoicing, only fearful dismay; when he died there was no grief or affliction, only a melancholy joy. In this fashion his life was passed, or, to speak more accurately, is passed, for this is not an ancient fairy tale that I am telling, of what has happened to an "individual" in bygone days. The same thing happens frequently. It lies close enough to us even though frivolity and sensuousness, worldly cleverness and godlessness wish to remain ignorant of it. It lies close enough to us even though they wish to keep away from any such unfortunate ones and to avoid all sober reminders not alone from the careless judgment of the storyteller's art, but also from the church and from the edifying insight that must certainly know that the Holy Scriptures have almost a predilection for the halt and the lame, the blind and the lepers. When the disciples began to seem "busy," Christ set a little child in their midst.[35] The crowd that storms and blusters in the bewildered name of the century might well tempt a serious man to set just such an unfortunate sufferer in their midst. The sight of him certainly would not detain anyone that willed anything eternal; but busyness has nothing whatever to do with the Eternal.

He, the sufferer, took part in life—by living. But to his life one thing was unknown, a thing which in all relations of life, as in the passion of love, makes for happiness: to be able to give and to receive "like for like." This "like for like" he never received, and he himself could never give; for as a sufferer he was always an object of sympathy and compassion. No, he never got like for like, not as a child, so that if others saddened his mother he might make her happy merely by smiling as he wakened. No, he never got like for like, for he loved his playmates in a different way than they loved him. No, he never got like for like, and therefore he got no mate. All through his life he could never do anything to repay others. And even in death he did not get like for like, for he was not mourned, as he had mourned those dear to him. He died, but what did the mourners and the priest say there except, "God be praised." Do not all these things cut him off from the highest?

Oh, you sufferer, wherever you may be, wherever you hide from the sight of men in order to spare them from being reminded of the pitiable, oh, do not forget that you, too, can accomplish something. Do not let your life consume itself in a futile counting up of the worthless sufferings of the days and years. Do not forget that you can accomplish something. If some feigned sufferer wishes to throw himself upon others because of a slight adversity, this does not mean that he should be told as is sometimes done, that he can accomplish something for others. For one who is capable of accomplishing something for others is not regarded by the edifying contemplation as in the strictest sense a sufferer. Instead he would be harsh with him. Oh, you true sufferer, even though your very suffer-

ing cuts you off from any such service to others, you can
still do—the highest thing of all. You can will to suffer
all and thereby be committed to the Good. Oh, blessed
justice, that the true sufferer can unconditionally do the
highest quite as well as fortune's favorite child! Honor
and praise be to the Eternal, in whom is no shadow of
turning, in whom is neither malice nor favoritism but
perfect justice. By willing to suffer all you are committed
to the Good, having changed your garments—yes, as when
the dead rise up and cast off their grave clothes, so you
have cast off the mantle of your misery. Now you are
indistinguishable from those whom you wish to be like—
those that are committed to the Good. All are clothed
alike, girded about the loins with truth, arrayed in the
armor of righteousness and wearing the helmet of salvation![36] If it be so, and it is the hope of every good man
that there is a resurrection where there shall be no difference, where the deaf man shall hear, the blind man
see, where he that bore a form of misery shall be fair like
all the others, then there is indeed on this side of the
grave some such resurrection each time a man, by willing
to do all or to suffer all, rises up by entering into the
commitment. and remains bound to the Good in the commitment. The sole difference is the pain of the wish in the
sufferer. But at the same time this may be a help to bring
him into the decision.

The sufferer must therefore be willing to suffer all. This
means equally to be willing to do all: to bring it to a commitment, to be and to remain loyal to the Good in the
commitment. While it is true that the pain of the wish is
the sign that the suffering in a way continues; yet the
healing also continues, as long as the sufferer remains firm
in the commitment. But there is a force that is momentarily
powerful. It is cleverness. From cleverness and from the

moment, or through it and from the moment, a man's destruction is born—if it is a fact that a man's salvation comes in the Eternal and by the Eternal. Now cleverness may be inwardly misused; for outwardly a true sufferer has little chance of misusing it. Cleverness in this inner realm is rich in evasions by which the time is put off and the decision is postponed. It will come to understand the decision only in an earthly and temporal sense. From its momentary standpoint, it has in view only a decision by which the suffering shall be brought to an end. But be assured, the Eternal does not heal in this fashion. The palsied man does not become whole, because he has been healed by the Eternal, nor the leper clean, nor the deformed made physically perfect. "But then it is a useless device, this help of the Eternal," cleverness suggests, "and what is still worse, is this decision, where the sufferer dedicates himself to his suffering, which indeed makes his condition hopeless"— because the decision renounces the juggling hope of temporal existence, Where the Eternal does not come to heal such a sufferer, what happens, with the aid of cleverness, is about as follows: first, the sufferer lives for some years by an earthly hope; but when this is exhausted and the suffering still continues, then he becomes superstitious, his state of health alternates between drowsiness and burning excitement. As the suffering continues, there settles over him finally a dull despair, broken only rarely by an unnatural and terribly enfeebling intensity, as when the gambler hopes on and on that some day he will meet with luck. Alas, at length a man sees what cleverness and this earthly hope amount to! For to cleverness it seems so clever "that one should not foolishly give up an earthly hope for a possible mythical healing"—in order to win the Eternal. To cleverness it seems so cunning "that one would not decide to say farewell to the earth; indeed, one can never know what possibly could happen . . . and then one would regret"—that one had let himself be healed by the Eternal. The earthly hope and the heavenly hope grew up well together and played together in childhood like born equals, but the difference reveals itself in the decision. Yet, this hinders cleverness which steadily hinders the decision. Those who cling to life put off the time, have countless inventions whose genius is this: that one must not take life and his own sorrows too much to heart, that it was just possible, who can know that—etc.

When the sufferer actually takes his suffering to heart, then he receives help from the Eternal toward his decision. Because to take one's suffering to heart is to be weaned from the temporal order, and from cleverness and from excuses, and from clever men and women and from anecdotes about this and that, in order to find rest in the blessed trustworthiness of the Eternal. For the sufferer, it is as if one should liken him to a sick man who turns himself from side to side, and now at last discovers the position in which there is relief—even if the wish still pains. Even if it was only a trifle, one can never have taken something too much to heart, when in taking it so to heart he thereby wins the Eternal.

But the sufferer who does not wish to be healed by the Eternal is double-minded. The double-mindedness in him is a disease that gnaws and gnaws and eats away the noblest powers; the injury is internal and infinitely more dangerous than being deformed and palsied. This double-minded one wishes to be healed and yet does not wish to be healed: eternally, he does not wish to be healed. But the temporal cure is uncertain, and the different stages in the scale of uncertainty are marked by increasing restlessness, in his double-mindedness. When the double-minded man comes to the final moment of his life, cleverness will still be sit-

ting at his deathbed and explaining that one cannot know
what might suddenly and unexpectedly happen. Under no
circumstances should a messenger be sent after the clergyman, for cleverness is so afraid of the decision that it even
regards the clergyman's coming as a tacit decision, and indeed one can never know what suddenly and unexpectedly
might happen. So the double-minded one dies, and now the
survivors know for certain that the deceased was not cured
of his long-standing suffering by any sudden and unex-
pected means. Alas, the Eternal is a riddle for the one who,
in the clever sense of the moment, loves the world. Over
and over again he thinks, what if some temporal help
should suddenly appear, then I would be trapped, I, who by
commitment to the Eternal had died to the temporal. He
prefers to say, one still regards the temporal as the highest,
one looks upon the Eternal as a kind of desperate "last
resort." Therefore, one objects to giving it the decision for
as long as possible. And even if temporal help is the most
absurd and unreasonable of all expectations, yet one would
sooner whip up his superstitious imagination to hope for
it than to lay hold on the Eternal. One is constantly afraid
that he might live to regret it, and yet the Eternal, if one
honestly lays hold on it, is the only thing, absolutely the
only thing of which it may be said without reservation, it
will never be regretted. But because of this fear that he
should one day regret committing himself to the Eternal,
a man deserves some day to be compelled to regret bitterly
that he allowed the time to pass by.

Oh, it is indeed a shallow cleverness (no matter how
much it brags or how loquacious it may be) that stupidly
cheats itself out of the highest consolation, getting along
with a mediocre and even less than mediocre consolation
and ending in inevitable remorse. Even if the sufferer is
able to use his cleverness in such a way as to give his dou-

ble-mindedness a little better public appearance than is de-·
picted here, that in no way affects the real situation. If he
uses cleverness to hinder commitment to the Eternal, he is
double-minded. He is, and he remains double-minded, even
if temporal help did come and he did revel in the cleverness
by which he had managed his shrewd escape; yes, one
should still believe that it was a calamity that he cleverly
managed to evade commitment to the Eternal. Commitment to the Eternal is the only true salvation. Therefore
it is also double-mindedness when the sufferer uses his
strength to conceal the pain instead of letting himself be
healed by the Eternal. Such a sufferer is not seeking release
from the suffering but only from a sympathy, in so far as
this also can be an affliction. Therein lies the contradictory
character of double-mindedness. For only by commitment
to the Eternal may he become really free from the painfulness of sympathy, since by the commitment he really over-
comes the suffering. Hence only the wish pains, while the
Eternal cures.

In relation to the sufferer, all double-mindedness has its
ground in and is marked by the double-minded one's un-
willingness to let go of the things of this world. In the
same way the double-minded talk that is from time to
time addressed to the sufferer may be recognized by the
fact that it puts its trust in the things of this world. It is
only too often the case that the sufferer shrinks from re-
ceiving the highest comfort, and the speaker is ashamed
to offer the highest consolation. Contrary to the truth, the
consoling talk seeks to offer comfort by saying that the illness will soon be better—perhaps; and begs for some little
patience. It coddles the sufferer a little, and says that by
Sunday all will surely be going well. Yet why give a pauper,
if we may for a moment compare the sufferer with a
pauper, silver or even counterfeit coin when one has a rich

supply of gold to offer him? For the Eternal's comfort is pure gold. Let us remember the active one even though his suffering is always different from that of a real sufferer. We read of the Apostles,[37] that when they were scourged they went on their way rejoicing and gave thanks to God. Here there is no talk of having a little patience, and of things going well by Sunday; but here is found the Eternal's victorious comfort, and these scourged Apostles have more than conquered. So, too, shall it be with the true sufferer. For when the Eternal heals, the wish continues to pain (for the Eternal does not remove the sufferer from time), but there is no whining, no temporary distraction, no deceitful evasion. One knows well enough that when the true sufferer has whined himself through time and by all kinds of imaginings has managed to pass away the time or to kill time: still eternity stands open to him. Alas, no, the true sufferer must also answer for the manner in which he has used his time, answer for whether or not he has used the earthly misery to allow himself eternally to be healed. But cleverness asserts, "still, one should never give up hope." "You hypocrite," answers the Eternal, "why do you speak so equivocally? You know well enough that there is a hope that should be put to death; that there is a lust and a desire and a longing that should be slain. Earthly hope should be put to death, for in just this way did man first come to be saved by the true hope." Therefore the sufferer should never be willing to "accept deliverance" (Hebrews 11:15) on this world's terms.

11. The Price of Willing One Thing:
The Sufferer's Use of Cleverness
to Expose Evasion

Bᴜᴛ *the sufferer who sincerely wills the Good,
uses this very cleverness to cut off evasions and hence to
launch himself into the commitment* and to escape the dis-
illusionments of choosing the temporal way. He does not
fear the mark of the commitment that, as it were, draws
the suffering over him; for he knows that this mark is the
breaking through of the Eternal. He knows that in the
commitment the nerve of the temporal order is being cut,
even though pain continues in the wish. There is no doubt
that what often makes a sufferer impatient is that he takes
upon himself in advance the suffering of a whole lifetime
and now quails before what would be lighter to bear if he
were to take each day's burden as it comes.

The commitment should not concentrate sufferings in
this way. For the error is just this, that in spite of all his
advance acceptance of suffering, the sufferer wins nothing
that is eternal but only becomes terrified in a temporal
sense. Because of the uncertainty of the temporal order,
it is also true that over a period of many years a sufferer
may talk himself out of the original impression of the commitment. And this is a calamity. On that account the sufferer who sincerely wills the Good knows that cleverness
is a treacherous friend, and that only the commitment is
fully trustworthy.

The active one will do all for the Good, the sufferer will
suffer all for the Good. The similarity is that they both may

be and remain committed to the Good. Only the direction
in which they work is different, and this difference must
not be understood as making them mutually exclusive. The
active one works from without in order that the Good may
conquer; even his suffering has significance from its bearing upon this goal. The true sufferer does everything inwardly (by being willing to suffer all) for the Good in
order that it may conquer in him. Yet the Good must have
conquered and must continue to conquer in the active one's
own heart, if he sincerely works for the Good outwardly.
The true sufferer can always work for the Good outwardly
by the power of example, and work effectually. For his
life, just because so much is denied him, contains a great
challenge to the many to whom much is given. His life
when he is and remains committed to the Good, contains a
severe judgment upon the many, who use in an inexcusable
way the much that has been given them. Yes, even if the
sufferer were denied this working by the power of example,
even if he were cut off from all other men, he would still
be sharing in mankind's great common concern. On his
lonely outpost he, too, would be defending a difficult pass
by saving his own soul from all of the ensnaring difficulties
of suffering. Although not a single man should see him,
mankind feels with him, suffers with him, and conquers
with him! For everywhere that the Good truly conquers,
the victory is really as great whether the Good conquers in
the many by means of one, or whether it conquers in a
solitary forsaken one by his own efforts; in reality the victory is equally great. Oh, praised be the blessed justice of
the Eternal!

Yet one thing still remains to be discussed before leaving the matter of sufferings: Can one be said to will suffering? Is not suffering something that one must be forced
into against his will? If a man can be free of it, can he

then will it, and if he is bound to it, can he be said to will it? If we would answer this question, let us first of all distinguish between what it is to will in the sense of inclination, and what it is to will in the noble sense of freedom. Yes, for many men it is almost an impossibility for them to unite freedom and suffering in the same thought. Hence, when they see a man of means who could spend his time easily and comfortably, when they see him straining himself as much as a scrupulous workman, exposing himself to many sufferings, choosing the burdensome way of a higher calling: they look upon him as either a fanatic or a lunatic. They all but complain that Providence has given all of these fortunate circumstances to someone that simply does not know how to make use of them. They think in their hearts even when they do not say it aloud, even when they do not consider how tragically they are betraying their own inner life: "We should have been there in his place, we should have really known how to enjoy that life." According to this, if one can be free of suffering it is either fanaticism or insanity to will it.

But what then is courage? Is it courage to go where pleasure beckons in order to see where pleasure is? Or, in order for courage to be revealed, is it not required that there be opposition (which even language seems to indicate) [38] as though the courageous person looks the danger in the eye, even though the danger is not what the eye wants to see? To illustrate, is it not as when the courageous knight spurs his horse forward against some terrifying object? There is no tremor of fear in his eye because courage controls even the expression of the eye. Yet the knight and the horse illustrate the structure of courage. The knight is the courageous one, the horse is skittish. The horse and its skittishness answer to that which is low in a man and its skittishness is that which courage checks. In this way, courage voluntarily wills suffering. The courageous one has a treacherous opposition within himself that is in league with the opposition without. But just on that account, he is the courageous one, because in spite of it he voluntarily wills the suffering.

On the other hand (and this is what we must primarily consider, for we are speaking of the true sufferer), the sufferer can voluntarily accept that suffering which in one sense is forced upon him, in so far as he does not have it in his power to get rid of it. Can anyone but one who is free of suffering, say, "Put me in chains, I am not afraid"? Can even a prisoner say, "Of my own free will I accept my imprisonment"—the very imprisonment which is already his condition? Here again the opinion of most men is that such a thing is impossible, and that therefore the condition of the sufferer is one of sighing despondency. But what then is patience?[39] Is patience not precisely that courage which voluntarily accepts unavoidable suffering? The unavoidable is just the thing which will shatter courage. There is a treacherous opposition in the sufferer himself that is in league with the dread of inevitability, and together they wish to crush him. But in spite of this, patience submits to suffering and by just this submission finds itself free in the midst of unavoidable suffering. Thus patience, if one may put it in this way, performs an even greater miracle than courage. Courage voluntarily chooses suffering that may be avoided; but patience achieves freedom in unavoidable suffering. By his courage, the free one voluntarily lets himself be caught, but by his patience the prisoner effects his freedom—although not in the sense that need make the jailer anxious or fearful.

The outward impossibility of ridding oneself of suffering does not hinder the inward possibility of being able really to emancipate oneself within suffering—of one's own free will accepting suffering, as the patient one gives his consent by willing to accept suffering. For one can be forced into the narrow prison, one can be forced into lifelong sufferings, and necessity is the tyrant; but one cannot be forced into patience. If the tyrant necessity presses upon a soul which neither possesses nor wills to possess the elasticity of freedom, then the soul becomes depressed, but it does not become patient. Patience is the counterpressure of resiliency, whereby the coerced ones are set free from restraint. Or can only the rich man be economical because he may, if he likes, be extravagant? Cannot the poor man also be economical even though he is powerless to be extravagant, even though he is forced to be—economical? No, he cannot be forced to be economical even though he is forced to be poor. Alas, the wisdom of many men seems calculated to abolish the Good. When a person of means voluntarily chooses the hard way, then he is called strange, "he who could be so well off without working and who could indulge his every desire for comfort." And when the victim of unavoidable suffering bears it patiently, one says of him, "to his shame, he is coerced, and he is making a virtue out of a necessity." Undeniably he is making a virtue out of a necessity, that is just the secret, that is certainly a most accurate designation for what he does. He makes a virtue out of necessity. He brings a determination of freedom out of that which is determined as necessity. And it is just there that the healing power of the decision for the Eternal resides: that the sufferer may voluntarily accept the compulsory suffering. Just as it is a relief to the sufferer to open himself in confidence to a friend, so it is deliverance to the sufferer to commit himself to the Eternal even though the compulsion of necessity should press against his heart, it is deliverance to open himself to the Eternal and to consent eternally to be willing to suffer all.

For that man is captive indeed for whom a door stands open: the trapdoor of eternity! And he is indeed in bonds, who is eternally free! When Paul said, "I am a Roman citizen,"[40] the prefect did not dare to put him into prison, and he was placed in voluntary confinement. In like fashion when a man dares declare, "I am eternity's free citizen," necessity cannot imprison him, except in voluntary confinement.

My listeners! If you are willing, let us recall the direction that our talk has taken. If a man should will one thing, then he must will the Good, for in this way alone was it possible for him to will a single thing. If, however, it is to be genuine, he must will the Good in truth. According to whether he is *an active one or a sufferer he must be willing either to do all for the Good, or he must be willing to suffer all for the Good*. He must be willing either to do all for the Good, or to be and to remain committed to the Good. But cleverness may be misused internally, to seek evasions; and misused externally in deception. The good man, on the contrary, uses cleverness to cut off all evasions and thereby to launch out and to remain constant—in the commitment. He also uses cleverness to prevent such external deception. He must be willing to suffer all for the Good, or to be and to remain committed to the Good. And the talk went on to describe the true sufferer's condition, because by looking at sufferings one may really learn what the highest is. Once again in regard to suffering, cleverness may be misused internally to seek ways of escape, but the Good man makes use of just this very cleverness against ways of escape, in order that he may be and remain committed to the Good, by being willing to suffer all, by accepting the enforced necessity of suffering.

But purity of heart is to will one thing. It is this thesis

that has been the object of the talk which we have linked to the apostolic words: "Draw nigh to God and he will draw nigh to you, cleanse your hands, ye sinners, and purify your hearts, ye double-minded!" For commitment to the Good is a whole-souled decision, and a man cannot by the craft and the flattery of his tongue lay hold of God while his heart is far away. No, for since God is spirit and truth, a man can only draw near to Him by sincerity, by willing to be holy, as He is holy:[41] by purity of heart. *Purity of heart:* it is a figure of speech that compares the heart to the sea, and why just to this? Simply for the reason that the depth of the sea determines its purity, and its purity determines its transparency. Since the sea is pure only when it is deep, and is transparent only when it is pure, as soon as it is impure it is no longer deep but only surface water, and as soon as it is only surface water it is not transparent. When, on the contrary, it is deeply and transparently pure, then it is all of one consistency, no matter how long one looks at it; then its purity is this constancy in depth and transparency. On this account we compare the heart with the sea, because the purity of the sea lies in its constancy of depth and transparency. No storm may perturb it; no sudden gust of wind may stir its surface, no drowsy fog may sprawl out over it; no doubtful movement may stir within it; no swift-moving cloud may darken it: rather it must lie calm, transparent to its depths. And today if you should see it so, you would be drawn upwards by contemplating the purity of the sea. If you saw it every day, then you would declare that it is forever pure—like the heart of that man who wills but one thing. As the sea, when it lies calm and deeply transparent, yearns for heaven, so may the pure heart, when it is calm and deeply transparent, yearn for the Good. As the sea is made pure by yearning for heaven alone; so may the heart become pure by yearning only for the Good. As the sea mirrors the elevation of heaven in its pure depths, so may the heart when it is calm and deeply transparent mirror the divine elevation of the Good in its pure depths. If the least thing comes in between, between the heavens and the sea, between the heart and the Good, then it would be sheer impatience to covet the reflection. For if the sea is impure it cannot give a pure reflection of the heavens.

12. What Then Must I Do?
The Listener's Role in a Devotional Address

My LISTENER! This talk was brought forth upon the occasion of the office of Confession. If after the opening references to this occasion no more has been said of it, yet it has never been forgotten in the talk. For what has been given is most intimately connected with what is appropriate to an address of invitation to such an occasion. From its single point of departure—*to will one thing*, the talk has moved out in different directions, ever returning, however, to this point of departure. It has at the same time scanned the earth, making note of human differences. From time to time it has depicted the individual error and the state of soul of one who has lost his way. This has been done on a magnified scale, so that man may the better become aware of, and look out for, what, in the trivial circumstances of daily life so rarely appears unmixed that it is much harder to detect than are these instances that are "writ large." As it has proceeded, the talk, holding tenaciously to the demand—*to will one thing*—has taught how to recognize many errors, disappointments, deceptions, and self-deceptions. It has striven to track down double-mindedness into its hidden ways, and to ferret out its secret. By striving at every possible point to make itself intelligible, the talk has sought to bring these things within the reach of each listener. But the intelligibility of the talk, and the listener's understanding of it, are still not the talk's true aim. This by no means gives the meditation its proper emphasis. For in order to achieve its proper emphasis the talk must unequivocally demand something of the listener. It must demand not merely what has previously been requested, that the reader should share in the work with the speaker—now the talk must unconditionally demand the reader's own decisive activity, and all depends upon this.

So, my listener, turn your attention now to the occasion, while consciousness of sin sharpens the need until it becomes the one thing necessary; while the earnestness of this holy place strengthens the will in holy determination, while the all-knowing One's presence makes self-deception impossible, consider your own life! The talk, which is without authority, will not have the presumption to pass judgment upon you. By vigorously pondering the occasion you will stand before a higher judge, where no man dares judge another since he himself is one of the accused. The talk does not address itself to you as if to a particularly designated person, for it does not know who you are. But if you weigh the occasion vigorously, then it will be to you, whoever you may be, it will be as if it spoke precisely to you. This is not due to any merit in the talk. It is the product of your own activity that for your own sake the talk is helpful to you; and it will be because of your own activity that you will be the one to whom the intimate "thou" is spoken. This is your own activity, it really is. Alas, above all let us not be drawn away from the decision by any attention to the speaker and the artistry of the talk. If this happens, then busyness and double-mindedness are again to blame that the emphasis in the composition is wrongly placed. In this case the devotional speaker is admired for his art, his eloquence, while that decision of which each man is capable, and that which it may be well to note, is the highest thing of all, is completely ignored. In a devotional sense, to be eloquent is a mere frill in the same way that to be beautiful is a happy privilege, but is still a non-essential frill. In a devotional sense, earnestness: to listen in order to act, this is the highest thing of all, and, God be praised, every man is capable of it if he so wills. Yet busyness places its most weighty emphasis upon the frills, the capacity to please, and looks upon earnestness as nothing at all. In a contemptuous and frivolous fashion, busyness thinks that to be eloquent is the highest thing of all and that the task of the listener is to pass judgment on whether the speaker has this gift.

In order that no irregularity may be admitted or no double-mindedness left unmentioned, let me then at this point, where the demand is being made for a person's own activity, briefly illustrate the relation between the speaker and the listener in a devotional address. Let me in order once again to take up arms against double-mindedness, make this illustration by borrowing a picture from worldly art. And do not let the two senses in which this may be taken disturb you or give you grounds for accusing the address of impropriety. For if you have dared to attend an exhibition of worldly art, then by doing this, you yourself must have come to understand what is meant by spiritual. Therefore you must have considered the spiritual with the worldly art even though it was the means of your first distinct recognition of the difference between the two. If you did not, discord and double-mindedness are in your own heart, so that you live for periods of time on the worldly plane with only an occasional thought of the spiritual. It is so on the stage, as you know well enough, that someone sits and prompts by whispers; he is the inconspicuous one, he is, and wishes to be overlooked. But then there is another, he strides out prominently, he draws every eye to himself. For that reason he has been given his name, that is: actor.[42] He impersonates a distinct individual. In the skillful sense of this illusory art, each word becomes true when embodied in him, true through him—and yet he is told what he shall say by the hidden one that sits and whispers. No one is so foolish as to regard the prompter as more important than the actor.

Now forget this light talk about art. Alas, in regard to things spiritual, the foolishness of many is this, that they in the secular sense look upon the speaker as an actor, and the listeners as theatergoers who are to pass judgment upon the artist. But the speaker is not the actor—not in the remotest sense. No, the speaker is the prompter. There are no mere theatergoers present, for each listener will be looking into his own heart. The stage is eternity, and the listener, if he is the true listener (and if he is not, he is at fault) stands before God during the talk. The prompter whispers to the actor what he is to say, but the actor's repetition of it is the main concern—is the solemn charm of the art. The speaker whispers the word to the listeners. But the main concern is earnestness: that the listeners by themselves, with themselves, and to themselves, in the silence before God, may speak with the help of this address.

The address is not given for the speaker's sake, in order that men may praise or blame him. The listener's repetition of it is what is aimed at. If the speaker has the responsibility for what he whispers, then the listener has an equally great responsibility not to fall short in his task. In the theater, the play is staged before an audience who are called theatergoers; but at the devotional address, God himself is present. In the most earnest sense, God is the critical theatergoer, who looks on to see how the lines are spoken and how they are listened to: hence here the customary audience is wanting. The speaker is then the prompter, and the listener stands openly before God. The listener, if I may say so, is the actor, who in all truth acts before God.

Oh, let us never forget this, let us not reduce the spiritual to the worldly. Even though we may earnestly think of the spiritual and the worldly together, let us forever distinguish between them. As soon as the spiritual is looked upon in worldly fashion (an observation for which one has the same foolishness to thank as that which would look upon the prompter in a play as more important than the actor) then the speaker becomes an actor and the listeners become critical theatergoers. In the same way, from the secular point of view, the devotional address is simply held for a group of attenders and God is no more present than he is in the theater. God's presence is the decisive thing that changes all. As soon as God is present, each man in the presence of God has the task of paying attention to himself. The speaker must see that during the address he pays attention to himself, to what he says; the listener, that during the address he pays attention to himself, to how he listens, and whether during the address he, in his inner self, secretly talks with God. If this were not done, then the listeners would be presuming to share God's task with him, God and the listeners together would

watch the speaker and pass judgment upon him. So it is
with the true relationship of speaker and listener in a devotional address.

Or to put it in another way, it is as if a subordinate
functionary of the church, who is without authority
should read aloud the prescribed prayer. Properly speaking, it is not the church functionary who prays. The one
who prays is the listener who sits in the church and opens
himself to God while he listens to the reading of the
prayer. Yet the listener does not speak, his voice is not
heard, nor does he pray softly to himself; but silently and
with his heart he is praying in the presence of God by
means of the audible voice of the one who reads out the
prayer, and whispers to him what he shall say. Yet this
is not earnestness: that one man shall tell another or dic-
tate to another what he shall say. But this *is* earnestness:
that the other man now should tell it to God speaking for
himself. Now we have come to a clear understanding about
this, and the demand will only be repeated in order that
the speaker may focus his mind actively upon the occasion
of the address.

The talk asks you, then, or you ask yourself by means
of the talk, *what kind of life do you live, do you will
only one thing, and what is this one thing?* The talk does
not expect that you will name off any goal that only
pretends to be one thing. For it does not intend to address itself to anyone with whom it would not be able
to deal seriously, for the reason that such a man has cut
himself off from any earnest consideration of the occasion
of the address. There is still another reason: a man can,
to be sure, have an extremely different, yes, have a precisely opposite opinion from ours, and one can nevertheless deal earnestly with him if one assumes that finally
there may be a point of agreement, a unity in some uni-

versal human sense, call it what you will. But if he is mad, then one cannot deal with him, for he shies away from just that final point, in which one at last may hope to find agreement with him. One can dispute with a man, dispute to the furthest limit, as long as one assumes, that in the end there is a point in common, an agreement in some universal human sense: in self-respect. But when, in his worldly strivings he sets out like a madman in a desperate attempt to despise himself, and in the face of this is brazen about it and lauds himself for his infamy, then one can undertake no disputing with him. For like a madman, and even more terribly, he shies away from this final thing (self-respect) in which one might at last hope to find agreement with him.

The talk assumes, then, that you will the Good and asks you now, *what kind of life you live, whether or not you truthfully will only one thing*. It does not ask inquisitively about your calling in life, about the number of workers you employ, or about how many you have under you in your office, or if you happen to be in the service of the state. No, the talk is not inquisitive. It asks you above all else, it asks you first and foremost, whether you really live in such a way that you are capable of answering that question, in such a way that the question truthfully exists for you. Because in order to be able earnestly to answer that serious question, a man must already have made a choice in life, he must have chosen the invisible, chosen that which is within. He must have lived so that he has hours and times in which he collects his mind, so that his life can win the transparency that is a condition for being able to put the question to himself and for being able to answer it—if, of course, it is legitimate to demand that a man shall know whereof he speaks. To put such a question to the man that is so busy in his earthly work, and outside of this in joining the crowd in its noisemaking, would be folly that would lead only to fresh folly—through the answer.

13. 𝔚𝔥𝔞𝔱 𝔗𝔥𝔢𝔫 𝔐𝔲𝔰𝔱 𝔍 𝔇𝔬?
Live as an "Individual"

THE TALK asks you, then, *whether you live in such a way that you are conscious of being an "individual."* The question is not of the inquisitive sort, as if one asked about that "individual" in some special sense, about the one whom admiration and envy unite in pointing out. No, it is the serious question, of what each man really is according to his eternal vocation, so that he himself shall be conscious that he is following it; and what is even more serious, to ask it as if he were considering his life before God. This consciousness is the fundamental condition for truthfully willing only one thing. For he who is not himself a unity is never really anything wholly and decisively; he only exists in an external sense—as long as he lives as a numeral within the crowd, a fraction within the earthly conglomeration. Alas, how indeed should such a one decide to busy himself with the thought: truthfully to will only one thing!

Indeed it is precisely this consciousness that must be asked for. Just as if the talk could not ask in generalities, but rather asks you as an individual. Or, better still, my listener, if you would ask yourself, whether you have this consciousness, whether you are actively contemplating the occasion of this talk. For in the outside world, the crowd is busy making a noise. The one makes a noise because he

heads the crowd, the many because they are members of
the crowd. But the all-knowing One, who in spite of
anyone is able to observe it all, does not desire the crowd.
He desires the individual; He will deal only with the individual, quite unconcerned as to whether the individual
be of high or low station, whether he be distinguished or
wretched.

Each man himself, as an individual, should render his
account to God. No third person dares venture to intrude
upon this accounting between God and the individual.
Yet the talk, by putting its question, dares and ought
to dare, to remind man, in a way never to be forgotten,
that the most ruinous evasion of all is to be hidden in
the crowd in an attempt to escape God's supervision of
him as an individual, in an attempt to get away from
hearing God's voice as an individual. Long ago, Adam
attempted this same thing when his evil conscience led
him to imagine that he could hide himself among the
trees. It may even be easier and more convenient, and
more cowardly to hide oneself among the crowd in the
hope that God should not be able to recognize one from
the other. But in eternity each shall render account as an
individual. That is, eternity will demand of him that he
shall have lived as an individual. Eternity will draw out
before his consciousness, all that he has done as an individual, he who had forgotten himself in noisy self-conceit.
In eternity, he shall be brought to account strictly as an
individual, he who intended to be in the crowd where
there should be no such strict reckoning. Each one shall
render account to God as an individual. The King shall
render account as an individual; and the most wretched
beggar, as an individual. No one may pride himself at
being more than an individual, and no one despondently
think that he is not an individual, perhaps because here

in earth's busyness he had not as much as a name, but
was named after a number.

For, after all, what is eternity's accounting other than
that the voice of conscience is forever installed with its
eternal right to be the exclusive voice? What is it other
than that throughout eternity an infinite stillness reigns
wherein the conscience may talk with the individual about
what he, as an individual, of what he has done of Good
or of evil, and about the fact that during his life he did
not wish to be an individual? What is it other than that
within eternity there is infinite space so that each person,
as an individual, is apart with his conscience? For in eternity there is no mob pressure, no crowd, no hiding place
in the crowd, as little as there are riots or street fights!
Here in the temporal order conscience is prepared to make
each person into an individual. But here in the temporal
order, in the unrest, in the noise, in the pressure of the
mob, in the crowd, in the primeval forest of evasion, alas,
it is true, the calamity still happens, that someone completely stifles the voice of his conscience—his conscience,
for he can never rid himself of it. It continues to belong
to him, or more accurately, he continues to belong to it.
Yet we are not now talking about this calamity, for even
among the better persons, it happens all too readily that
the voice of conscience becomes merely one voice among
many. Then it follows so easily that the isolated voice of
conscience (as generally happens to a solitary one) becomes overruled—by the majority. But in eternity, conscience is the only voice that is heard. It must be heard
by the individual, for the individual has become the eternal
echo of this voice. It must be heard. There is no place to
flee from it. For in the infinite there is no place, the individual is himself the place. It must be heard. In vain
the individual looks about for the crowd. Alas, it is as

if there were a world between him and the nearest individual, whose conscience is also speaking to him about
what *he* as an individual has spoken, and done, and thought
of good and of evil.

Do you now live so that you are conscious of yourself
as an individual; that in each of your relations in which
you come into touch with the outside world, you are
conscious of yourself, and that at the same time you are
related to yourself as an individual? Even in these relations which we men so beautifully style the most intimate
of all, do you remember that you have a still more intimate relation, namely, that in which you as an individual
are related to yourself before God? If you are bound to
another human being by the holy bond of matrimony,
do you consider in this intimate relation that still more
intimate relation in which you as an individual are related
to yourself before God? The talk does not ask you whether
you now love your wife: it hopes so; nor whether she is
the apple of your eye and the desire of your heart: it
wishes you this. It does not ask what you have done to
make your wife happy, about how you both have ar-
ranged your household life, about what good advice you
have been able to get from others, or what harmful influence others have had upon you. It does not ask whether
your marital life is more commendable than that of many
others, or whether it perhaps might be looked upon by
some as a worthy example. No, the talk asks about none
of these things. It asks you neither in congratulation, nor
inquisitively, nor watchfully, nor apologetically, nor comparatively. It asks you only about the ultimate thing:
whether you yourself are conscious of that most intimate
relation to yourself as an individual. You do not carry the
responsibility for your wife, nor for other men, nor by
any comparative standard with other men, but only as an

individual, before God, where it is not asked whether your marriage was in accordance with others, with the common practice, or better than others, but where you as an individual will be asked only whether it was in accordance with your responsibility as an individual. For common practice changes, and all comparison goes lame, or is only half truth. But eternity's practice, which never goes out of fashion, is, that you are the individual, that you yourself in the intimate relation of marriage should have been conscious of this.

In truth, it is not divorce that eternity is aiming at, neither is it divorce, that eternity does away with the difference between man and woman. Your wife will have no occasion to grieve because you are pondering this, your most intimate relation to God. And should she be so foolish as to desire for herself only that which is earthly or even foolish enough to desire as well to draw you down to the earthly: yet a woman's folly shall certainly not be able to change the law of eternity. In eternity it will not be asked whether your wife seduced you (eternity will talk with her about that), but simply as an individual you will be asked whether you allowed yourself to be seduced. If your marriage is so blessed that you see a family growing up around you, may you be conscious that while you have an intimate relation to your children you have a still more intimate relation to yourself as an individual. You share the responsibility with your wife, and hence eternity will also ask her as an individual about her share of the responsibility. For in eternity there is not a single complication that is able to make the accounting difficult and evasion easy. Eternity does not ask concerning how far you brought up your children in the way that you saw others do it. It simply asks you, as an individual, how you brought up your children. It does not talk with you

in the manner that you would talk with a friend in confidence. For alas, even this confidence can all too easily
accustom you to evasions. For even the most trustworthy
friend still speaks as a third person. And by much of such
confidence, one easily gets used to speaking of himself as
if he were a third person. But in eternity, you are the
individual, and conscience when it talks with you is no
third person, any more than you are a third person when
you talk with conscience. For you and conscience are one.
It knows all that you know, and it knows that you know
it. With respect to your children's upbringing you can
weigh various matters with your wife, or your friends.
But how you act and the responsibility for it is finally
wholly and solely yours as an individual. And if you fail
to act, hiding from yourself and from others behind a
screen of deliberation, you bring down the responsibility
solely upon yourself as an individual.

Yes, in the temporal order where in all directions both
this and that are asked about in the manifold complex
complications of their reciprocal action, there one may
rightly enough believe that it was a fantasy of the imagination, a chimera, that each one among these countless
millions of people should be convinced accurately down
to the least trifle of what his life consisted. But in eternity
this is possible, because each becomes an individual. And
this applies to every relation of your life.

If you do not live in some out-of-the-way place in the
world, if you live in a populous city, and you direct your
attention outwards, sympathetically engrossing yourself in
the people and in what is going on, do you remember each
time you throw yourself in this way into the world around
you, that in this relation, you relate yourself to yourself
as an individual with eternal responsibility? Or do you
press yourself into the crowd, where the one excuses him-

self with the others, where at one moment there are, so
to speak, many, and where in the next moment, each time
that the talk touches upon responsibility, there is no one?
Do you judge like the crowd, in its capacity as a crowd?
You are not obliged to have an opinion about what you
do not understand. No, on the contrary, you are eternally
excused from that. But you are eternally responsible as
an individual to render an account for your opinion, and
for your judgment. And in eternity, you will not be asked
inquisitively and professionally, as though by a newspaper
reporter, whether there were many that had the same—
wrong opinion. You will be asked only whether you have
held it, whether you have spoiled your soul by joining in
this frivolous and thoughtless judging, because the others,
because the many judged thoughtlessly. You will be asked
only whether you may not have ruined the best within
you by joining the crowd in its defiance, thinking that
you were many and therefore you had the prerogative,
because you were many, that is, because you were many
who were wrong. In eternity it will be asked whether you
may not have damaged a good thing, in order that you
also might judge with them that did not know how to
judge, but who possessed the crowd's strength, which in
the temporal sense is significant but to which eternity is
wholly indifferent.

You see, in the temporal order, a man counts and says:
"One more or less, it makes no difference"—and he applies
this even to himself! In the temporal order a man counts
and says: "One over against a hundred, after all what
can come of that?" So he grows cowardly in the face of
—number. And numbers are usually false. Truth is content to be a unity. But a man wins something by this
cowardly indulgence. He does not win a bed in a hospital.
No, but he wins the amazing thing of becoming the

strongest of all, because the crowd is always the strongest.
Eternity, on the other hand, never counts. The individual
is always only one and conscience in its meticulous way
concerns itself with the individual. In eternity you will
look in vain for the crowd. You will listen in vain to
find whether you cannot hear where the noise and the
gathering is, so that you may run to it. In eternity you,
too, will be forsaken by the crowd. And this is terrifying.
Yet in the temporal order to be forsaken by the crowd,
provided that the Eternal comforts, may be something
blessed, and the pain of it, a mere jest. What then in
eternity will conscience demand of you by the consciousness that you are an individual? It will teach you that if
you judge (for in very many cases it will restrain you from
judging), you must bear the responsibility for your judgment. It will teach you that you should examine what
you understand and what you do not understand as if
you stood trembling in the presence of a departed one;
it wishes to frighten you from resorting to the brilliant
flights into wretchedness to which you are often subject.
For many fools do not make a wise man, and the crowd
is doubtful recommendation for a cause. Yes, the larger
the crowd, the more probable that that which it praises
is folly, and the more improbable that it is truth, and the
most improbable of all that it is any eternal truth. For
in eternity crowds simply do not exist. The truth is not
such that it at once pleases the frivolous crowd—and at
bottom it never does; to such a multitude the truth must
appear as simply absurd. But the man who, conscious of
himself as an individual, judges with eternal responsibility,
he is slow to pass judgment upon the unusual. For it is
possible that it is falsehood and deceit and illusion and
vanity. But it is also possible that it is true. He remembers
the word of the simple sage of ancient times: "This, that

a man's eye cannot see by the light by which the majority see could be because he is used to darkness; but it could also be because he is used to a still clearer light, and when this is so, it is no laughing matter."[43]

No, it is no laughing matter, but it is laughable, or it is pitiable, that the frivolous ones laugh at a man because he is wiser or better than they. For even laughter calls for a reasonable ground, and when this is absent, the laughter becomes the very thing that is laughable. But here in the temporal order, in the midst of earth's appalling prodigality with human beings, here number tempts. It tempts a man to count, to count himself in with the crowd. Here, by the use of round numbers, everything can be manipulated with ease. Yes, here in the temporal order it is possible that no individual can ever succeed, even if it were true that he sincerely willed the Good, in dispersing the crowd. But eternity can do it. Eternity seizes each one by the strong arm of conscience, holding him as an individual. Eternity sets him apart with his conscience. Woe unto him, if he is left to this judge alone! For in that case eternity will set him apart with his conscience in that place where there is pressure, to be sure, but not as in the temporal order where the pressure is the excuse, yes, the victory. No, eternity places him where to be under pressure is to be alone, stripped of every excuse; to be alone and to be lost. The royal psalm singer says that: while the heathen clamor, God sits in his heaven and laughs at them.[44] I dare not believe this. It would seem to be preferable to say that: while the crowd clamors and shouts and triumphs and celebrates; while one individual after another hastens to the place of tumult, where it is good to be if one is in search of oblivion and indulgence from that which is eternal; while at the same time the crowd shouts mockingly at God, "Yes, now see

whether you can get hold of us"; yet since it is difficult
in the rush of the crowd to distinguish the individual,
difficult to see the single tree when one is looking at the
wood, the sober countenance of eternity quietly waits. And
if all the generations that have lived on earth rose up and
gathered themselves in a single crowd in order to loose a
storm against eternity, in order to coerce eternity by their
colossal majority: eternity would scatter them as easily as
the firmness of an immovable rock would scatter frothy
scum; as easily as the wind when it rushes forward scatters
chaff. Just as easily, but not in the same way. For the wind
scatters the chaff, but then turns around and drifts it
together again. Eternity scatters the crowd by giving each
an infinite weight, by making him heavy—as an individual.
For what in eternity is the highest blessing is also the
deepest seriousness. What, there, is the most blessed comfort, is also the most appalling responsibility.

In eternity there are chambers enough so that each may
be placed alone in one. For wherever conscience is present,
and it is and shall be present in each person, there exists
in eternity a lonely prison, or the blessed chamber of salvation. On that account this consciousness of being an
individual is the primary consciousness in a man, which is
his eternal consciousness. But that man is slow to pass
judgment who bears in mind, that he is an individual,
and that the final and highest responsibility for the judgment rests solely upon him. For even the most trusted
friend in passing judgment as an impartial observer must
necessarily leave out what is crucial. To be the party directly concerned, the one to whom conscience in this affair
speaks the intimate "thou," is another matter, for conscience only speaks this intimate "thou" to your friend in
regard to the manner in which he is to give counsel. Such
a thoughtful one does not willingly pass judgment on

many things, and just this helps him to will only one thing.
He thinks it is not altogether an advantage to live in a
populous city where because of the swiftness of the means
of communication almost everyone can easily have a hasty
and superficial judgment about everything possible. On
the contrary, he looks upon this easiness as a temptation
and a snare and he learns earnestness in order as an individual to be concerned about his eternal responsibility.

"Even a fool might be a wise man if he could keep
silent," says the proverb.[45] And this is so, not merely because then he would not betray his foolishness, but also
because this self-control would help him to become conscious of himself as an individual, and would prevent him
from adopting the crowd's opinion. Or if he had an
opinion of his own, it would prevent him from hastening
to get the crowd to adopt it. The one who is conscious
of himself as an individual has his vision trained to look
upon everything as inverted. His sense becomes familiar
with eternity's true thought: that everything in this life
appears in inverted form. The purely momentary, in the
next moment, to say nothing of eternity, becomes nonsense
and vanity: the fiery moment of lust (and what is so
strong for the moment as lust!) is loathsome in memory;
the fiery moment of anger, revenge, and passion whose
gratification seems an irresistible impulse is horrible to remember. For the angry one, the vengeful one, the passionate one, thinks in the moment of passion that he re-
venges himself. But in the moment of remembrance, when
the act of revenge comes back to him, he loathes himself,
for he sees that precisely in that moment of revenge he
lost himself. The purely momentary seems to be profitable.
Yet in the next moment its deception becomes apparent
and, eternally understood, calls for repentance. So it is
with all things of the moment, and hence with the crowd's

opinion or with membership in the crowd in so far as this opinion and this membership is a thing of the moment.

My listeners, do you at present live in such a way that you are yourself clearly and eternally conscious of being an individual? This was the question the address was to ask, or rather that you are to ask yourself, if you actively consider this occasion. The talk should not tell you only that which will disturb you, even though many are of the conviction that a man ought ever to live in such an aroused state of consciousness. Nor is it concerned how many or how few hold that conviction. The speaker will not attempt to win you to this conviction, even if he does as a rule hold it himself. He does not wish to force it upon you any more than you would desire to force it upon him if you were of this conviction. For the exalted earnestness of the Eternal wishes neither the commendation of the majority nor the commendation of eloquence. One thing alone the talk does not dare to promise you—nor does it wish to insult you. It does not dare to promise you earthly gain if you enter upon and in dedication persevere in this conviction. On the contrary, if persevered in, it will make your life more taxing, and frequently perhaps wearisome. If persevered in, it may make you the target of others' ridicule, not to mention even greater sacrifices that perseverance might choose to require of you. Of course, the ridicule does not distract you if you continue to persist in your conviction. Ridicule will even be a help to you, in the sense that it is a further proof to you that you are on the right path. For the judgment of the crowd has its significance. One should not remain proudly ignorant of it, no, one should be attentive to it. If after this he sees to it that he does the opposite from the judgment of the crowd, then he, for the most part, does the right thing. Or if at the outset a man does the opposite, and he is then so fortunate as to have the judgment of the crowd express itself to the contrary, then he can be fairly certain that he has laid hold of the right thing. Then he has not only himself inwardly weighed and tested the conviction properly, but he has also the advantage of having it tested a second time by the help of ridicule. Ridicule may wound his feelings but just by that wound it shows that he is on the right path—the path of honor and of victory, like a warrior's wound, when it is on the breast where both the wound and the badge of honor are to be borne.

You have surely noticed among schoolboys, that the one that is regarded by all as the boldest is the one who has no fear of his father, who dares to say to the others, "Do you think I am afraid of him?" On the other hand, if they sense that one of their number is actually and literally afraid of his father, they will readily ridicule him a little. Alas, in men's fear-ridden rushing together into a crowd (for why indeed does a man rush into a crowd except because he is afraid!) there, too, it is a mark of boldness not to be afraid, not even of God. And if someone notes that there is an individual outside the crowd who is really and truly afraid—not of the crowd, but of God, he is sure to be the target of some ridicule. The ridicule is usually glossed over somewhat and it is said: a man should *love* God.

Yes, to be sure, God knows that man's highest consolation is that God is love and that man is permitted to love Him. But let us not become too forward, and foolishly, yes, blasphemously, dismiss the tradition of our fathers, established by God Himself: that really and truly a man should fear God. This fear is known to the man who is himself conscious of being an individual, and thereby is conscious of his eternal responsibility before

God. For he knows, that even if he could with the help of
evasions and excuses, get on well in this life, and even if
he could by this shady path have gained the whole world,
yet there is still a place in the next world where there is
no more evasion than there is shade in the scorching desert.

The talk will not go into this further. It will only ask
you again and again, do you now live so that you are
conscious of being an individual and thereby that you
are conscious of your eternal responsibility before God?
Do you live in such a way that this consciousness is able
to secure the time and quiet and liberty of action to penetrate every relation of your life? This does not demand
that you withdraw from life, from an honorable calling,
from a happy domestic life. On the contrary, it is precisely that consciousness which will sustain and clarify
and illuminate what you are to do in the relations of life.
You should not withdraw and sit brooding over your eternal accounting. To do this is to deserve something further
to account for. You will more and more readily find time
to perform your duty and your task, while concern over
your eternal responsibility will hinder you from being
"busy" and busily having a hand in everything possible
—an activity that can best be called: time-wasting.

14. What Then Must I Do?

Occupation and Vocation; Means and End

THIS WAS the principal question. For as only one
thing is necessary, and as the theme of the talk is the
willing of only one thing: hence the consciousness before

God of one's eternal responsibility to be an individual is
that one thing necessary. The talk now asks further,
"*What is your occupation in life?*" The talk does not ask
inquisitively about whether it is great or mean, whether
you are a king or only a laborer. It does not ask, after
the fashion of business, whether you earn a great deal of
money or are building up great prestige for yourself. The
crowd inquires and talks of these things. But whether your
occupation is great or mean, is it of such a kind that you
dare think of it together with the responsibility of eternity? Is it of such a kind that you dare to acknowledge
it at this moment or at any time? Suppose that something
terrible happened; suppose that the city in which you live
suddenly perished like those cities in the far south, and
everything came to rest, each one standing in his once-
chosen occupation. But suppose this happened without the
excuse of "being in practical harmony with the commonly
accepted customs of his age," the excuse pronounced by
a later generation, in order to shield you from disgrace!
Or what is still more serious, suppose one of the most
eminent dead, one whose memory the masses keep green,
as is their custom, by noisy festivities and by shouting;
suppose such a one should come to you. Suppose he visited
you and that you there before him, before his piercing
gaze, dared continue in your present occupation! Are you
not used to thoughts of this kind? It is in just such a way
that the transfigured one might well wish to serve after
death: by visiting the individual. For it must certainly
fill them with disgust if, in their blessed dwelling place,
they should become aware that a frivolous crowd treats
the transfigured dead as only a living fool could wish to
be treated: paying them honor by noisemaking and hand-
clapping. Do not think, that the transfigured one has become an aristocrat. On the contrary, he has become even

more humble, more humanly sympathetic with each man. Hence when, like a superior official, he travels on his visits to individuals, he will not reject the meanest occupation, if it is truly honorable. Oh, in eternity where he dwells, all trivial differences are forgotten. But the transfigured one, like eternity, does not desire the crowd. He desires the individual. On that account, if you should ever be almost ashamed of your mean occupation, because, among the world's distinctions, it is so mean, the transfigured one's visit to you as an individual will give you the courage of frankness. The transfigured one's visit to you as an individual will give you that courage of frankness—but what am I speaking of—and if you actively consider the occasion of this talk, then you will stand as an individual before a still more exalted one who, none the less, thinks still more humanly—about the meanness of the occupation, but also infinitely more purely about which occupation is truly honorable.

In your occupation, what is your attitude of mind? And how do you carry out your occupation? Have you made up your own mind that your occupation is your real calling so that you do not have to make explanation hinge on the result, maintaining that it was not your real calling if the results are not favorable, if your efforts do not succeed? Alas, such fickleness weakens a man immeasurably. Therefore persevere. By God's help and by your own faithfulness something good will come from the unpromising beginning. For there are beginnings everywhere, and there are good beginnings, where you begin with God; and no day is the wrong one to begin upon—not even an unpromising one, if you begin with God.

Or have you let yourself be deceived into regarding something as your calling because it turned out well, because it brought immediate success, perhaps even remarkable success? Alas, it is actually said in the world, often enough even by those who think they speak piously: "The proof that a man's occupation is the right one is that he is able to practice it." As if, because a man *could* so harden his heart that he could placidly practice all manner of cruelty, then this was what he ought to do. As if, because this brazen one could find the most hideous atrocity in his heart, and was able to carry it out, then this was the thing he ought to do! No, an unfavorable result can no more disprove the faithful man's conviction of what his calling should be, than a favorable result can of itself prove that he is in his proper calling.

Are you of one mind about the manner in which you will carry out your occupation, or is your mind continually divided because you wish to be in harmony with the crowd? Do you stand firmly behind your offer, not obstinately, not sullenly, but eternally concerned; do you continue unchanged to bid for the same thing and continue in your wish to buy the same thing even though the terms have been altered in a number of respects? Do you think that the Good is no different from gold, that it can be bought too dearly? Is there any profit you could not do without for the sake of the Good, any distinction you could not give up, any relation you could not renounce? Is there any stamp of approval from above that is any more important than this to you or perhaps some approbation from below? If you think that the Good must be bought at any price, then will you become envious when you see others buying for a lower price, that which you had to buy so dearly—but which, and do not forget this, is worth any price? If your endeavor succeeds, are you then conscious that you are an unprofitable servant; so that the reward does not affect you, as though you became more useful because you got a reward; and adversity does not affect you, since it merely expresses, what you shamefacedly will admit—that you have no right to claim anything? Hide nothing away suspiciously in your soul as though you still wished that it had happened differently, so that you might be able to pounce upon the reward as if it were prey, might be able to assume credit for it, might be able to point to it; as though you wished that adversity did not exist because it constrains the selfish thing in you that, even though repressed, foolishly makes you imagine that if you had luck with you, then you might do something for the Good, something that was worth talking about. Never forget that the devout wise man wishes no stroke of adversity to be taken away when it comes his way, because he cannot know whether or not it may be good for him. Never forget that the devout wise man wins his most beautiful of all victories, when the powerful one who had persecuted him wishes, so to speak, to release him, and the wise man replies: "I cannot unconditionally wish to be released, for I cannot know for certain that the persecution might not be good for me." Do you do good only out of fear of punishment, so that you scowl, even when you will the Good, so that in your dreams at night, you wish away the punishment and to that extent also the Good, and in your dreams by day imagine that one can with a slavish mind serve the Good? Oh, the Good is no difficult master, that wills one thing today, and another tomorrow. The Good always wishes one and the same thing. But it reckons with exactness and can be that which demands sincerity and can see whether it is present!

And now the means that you use. What means do you use in order to carry out your occupation? Are the means as important to you as the end, wholly as important? Otherwise it is impossible for you to will only one thing,

for in that case the irresponsible, the frivolous, the self-
seeking, and the heterogeneous means would flow in between in confusing and corrupting fashion. Eternally
speaking, there is only one means and there is only one
end: the means and the end are one and the same thing.
There is only one end: the genuine Good; and only one
means: this, to be willing only to use those means which
genuinely are good—but the genuine Good is precisely
the end. In time and on earth one distinguishes between
the two and considers that the end is more important than
the means. One thinks that the end is the main thing
and demands of one who is striving that he reach the
end. He need not be so particular about the means. Yet
this is not so, and to gain an end in this fashion is an
unholy act of impatience. In the judgment of eternity the
relation between the end and the means is rather the reverse of this.

If a man sets himself a goal for his endeavor here in
this life, and he fails to reach it, then, in the judgment
of eternity, it is quite possible that he may be blameless.
Yes, he may even be worthy of praise. He might have
been prevented by death, or by an adversity that is beyond
his control: in which case he is entirely without blame.
He might even have been prevented from reaching the
goal just by being unwilling to use any other means than
those which the judgment of eternity permits. In which
case by his very renunciation of the impatience of passion
and the inventions of cleverness, he is even worthy of
praise. He is not, therefore, eternally responsible for
whether he reaches his goal within this world of time.
But without exception, he is eternally responsible for the
kind of means he uses. And when he will only use or
only uses those means which are genuinely good, then, in
the judgment of eternity, he is at the goal. If reaching the

goal should be the excuse and the defense for the use of illicit or questionable means—alas, suppose he should die tomorrow. Then the clever one would be caught in his own folly. He had used illicit means, and he died before reaching the goal. For reaching the goal comes at the conclusion; but using the means comes at the beginning. Reaching the goal is like hitting the mark with his shot; but using the means is like taking aim. And certainly the aim is a more reliable indication of the marksman's goal than the spot the shot strikes. For it is possible for a shot to hit the mark by accident. The marksman may also be blameless if the shell does not go off. But no irregularities of the aim are permissible. To the temporal and earthly passion the end is unconditionally more important than the means. On that very account, it is the passionate one's torment, which if carried to its height must indeed make him sleepless and then insane, namely, that he has no control over time, and that he continually arrives too late, even if it was by merely half an hour. And what is still worse, since earthly passion is the rule, it can truthfully be said, that it is not wisdom which saves the worst ones from going insane, but indolence. On the other hand, the blessed comfort of the Eternal is like a refreshing sleep, is like "the cold of snow in the time of harvest"[46] to the one who wills the Eternal. He whose means are invariably just as important as the end, never comes too late. Eternity is not curious and impatient as to what the outcome in this world of time will be. It is just because of this that the means are without exception as important as the end. To earthly and worldly passion, this observation must seem shocking and paralyzing. To it conscience must seem the most paralyzing thing of all. For conscience is indeed "a blushing innocent spirit that sets up a tumult in a man's breast and fills him with difficulties" just because to conscience the means are without exception as important as the end.

Therefore, my listeners, in the carrying out of your occupation, which we have assumed to be something good and honorable, are the means without exception as important to you as the end? Or have your thoughts become giddy until the greatness of the goal made you look upon illicit means as of negligible importance? Alas, this state of giddiness is to be found least of all in eternity, for eternity is clear and transparent! Do you think that the greatness of an achievement makes it unnecessary for it to ask about a trivial wrong, that is, do you think that a wrong might exist which would be something of no significance, although as an obligation it is infinitely more important than the greatest achievement! Do you think that it is immaterial the way in which a masterpiece is produced? Well, perhaps that might hold for a masterpiece. But do you think that the master dares to be unconcerned about whether he piously consecrates his powers in holy service, or whether by despair in the midst of glittering sins he simply produces—a masterpiece?

And if the thought does not make you giddy, if you are sober and alert, are you particular in every respect in your use of the means? If a youth (and he is also a blushing and innocent spirit) should turn to you, do you dare without exception to let him know all? In your whole conduct is there not something, yes, how shall I express it, I could describe it at length but I would rather put it briefly in this fashion: is there not something, of which you could be fairly certain that the older people and those of your own age would almost admire for its cleverness and ingenuity if you told them of it, but which, strangely enough, a youth would blush over (not over your being so clever, but over your not being big enough to despise acting so cleverly)? Perhaps it is by flattery that you had won over this person and that, by concealing something, won this or that advantage, by a little untruth made a glittering trade, by a false union promoted your cause. Perhaps you had won the victory by allying yourself with admiration based upon a misunderstanding, had won riches and power by clever scheming to enter into the smartest combination. In your whole conduct, open and secret, is there not something that you would not for any price consent to let a youth discover (and it is beautiful that you love the youth so much and wish to guard his purity!)? Is there not something—against yourself—that you can still be willing to admit yourself to be guilty of? Something that you would not for any price confide to a youth? Yet, as I have told you, if you actively consider the occasion of this talk, then you stand before a higher judge, who judges infinitely more purely than the purest innocence of youth; a judge, that you will not out of indulgence let into the secret of your guilt, for He already knows you.

And what is your attitude toward others? Are you at one with all—by willing only one thing? Or do you contentiously belong to a party, or is your hand raised against every man and every man's hand raised against you? Do you wish for all others what you wish for yourself, or do you desire the highest thing of all for you and yours, or do you desire that that which you and yours desire shall be the highest thing of all? Do you do unto others what you will that they should do unto you—by willing only one thing? For this will is the eternal order that governs all things, that brings you into union with the dead, and with the men whom you never see, with foreign people whose language and customs you do not know, with all men upon the whole earth, who are related to each other by blood and eternally related to the Divine by eternity's task of willing only one thing. Do you wish, that there should be another law for you and yours than for the others? Do you wish to find your consolation in something other than that in which each man without exception may and shall find consolation?

Suppose that sometime a king and a beggar and a man like yourself should come to you. In their presence would you dare frankly to confess that that which you desire in the world, in which you sought your consolation, certain that the king in his majesty would not despise you even though you were a man of inferior rank; certain that the beggar would not go away envious that he could not have the same consolation; certain that the man like yourself would be pleased by your frankness? Alas, there is something in the world called clannishness. It is a dangerous thing because all clannishness is divisive. It is divisive when clannishness shuts out the common citizen, and when it shuts out the nobleborn, and when it shuts out the civil servant. It is divisive when it shuts out the king, and when it shuts out the beggar, and when it shuts out the wise man, and when it shuts out the simple soul. For all clannishness is the enemy of universal humanity. But to will only one thing, genuinely to will the Good, as an individual, to will to hold fast to God, which things each person without exception is capable of doing, this is what unites. And if you sat in a lonely prison far from all men, or if you were placed out upon a desert island with only animals for company, if you genuinely will the Good, if you hold fast to God, then you are in unity with all men. And if the terrible thing happened (for religious edification should not, like a woman's finery be intended for a splendid moment) that you were buried alive, if, as you awakened in the coffin you seized upon your accustomed consolation, then even in this lonely torment, you would be in unity with all men. Is this your present attitude? Have you no special privilege, no special talent, none of life's special favors that, either separately or in company with some others, vanity has led you to take, so that you could console yourself by means of it, and that makes you dare not tell the uninitiated the source of your consolation? Thus you give alms to the poor man so that he can console himself, but treacherously you have a further consolation for yourself. To be sure, you give a consolation for poverty, but you console yourself by the fact that your wealth assures you against ever becoming poor. You help to set the simple ones right, but treacherously you have a further consolation for yourself; your talent is so outstanding, that it could never happen that when you awakened tomorrow you were the stupidest person in all the land. You wish to instruct the youth, but you do not have the heart to take him into your confidence, because you have a secret of your own, because you are a traitor who deceived youth as to what was the highest thing of all by your secret, and deceived yourself as to what was the highest thing of all—by your secret!

And now a question concerning the sufferer. It is not a question of the state of his health. No, the talk is not sympathetic in this respect. Oh, but if you actively consider the occasion of this talk, then by being in the presence of God you would raise yourself above human sympathy. Then you would no longer pine wretchedly for sympathy. For although it happens all too seldom, if this could properly be proved to you, as you may well wish that it might, then with cheerful frankness you could give thanks for it. You would not give thanks bent over like a beggar—God would prevent that. And if sympathy is denied you, if a man is afraid, and in a selfish and cowardly manner avoids, yes, almost loathes you because he does not dare to think of your suffering, then you should be able to do without sympathy. You should not feel bitter over this lack of sympathy—God will take care of that. The talk asks you then, or you ask yourselves by means of the talk, whether you now live in such a way that you truthfully will only one thing. It is not the intention of the talk to presume to judge of this, far from it. The talk judges no one. Even the Holy Scriptures have an especially tender love for the unfortunate ones. Indeed it is particularly appropriate for a devotional meditation to concern itself principally with the sufferer, just as one in the world addresses the powerful man, the distinguished man. The talk does not ask inquisitively and busily about the name of your particular suffering, about how many years it has continued, about what the doctor or the pastor thinks, how much earthly hope they give you. Alas, out of vanity, sufferings, too, can in this fashion be taken as a mark of distinction that draws the attention of others to oneself.

So on that account, see that you question yourself by means of the talk. If the sufferer talks to himself in private, asks himself which kind of life he leads, whether he truthfully wills only one thing: then he is not tempted to relate in detail what he himself knows best of all, he is not tempted to compare. For all comparison injures. Yes, it is evil. Do you at present genuinely will only one thing? You know that if the only reason you will but one thing is that by this, and by this alone, you will be set free from suffering, then you do not genuinely will but one thing. But even if you could so dull yourself that the wish would die out, so that you could sever the wish's painful tie with that happier sense of being a man, of loving to live, of loving to be a happy one, still you would fail to

will only one thing. What at present is your condition in
suffering? The doctor and the pastor ask about your
health, but eternity makes *you* responsible for your condition. Is it so that it does not frivolously or superstitiously
fluctuate in a fever of impatience? Is it so that it is not a
dismally sluggish painlessness? Or is it so that you are willing to suffer all and let the Eternal comfort you? As time
goes by, how does your condition change? Did you begin
well perhaps but become more and more impatient? Or
perhaps you were impatient at the beginning, but learned
patience from what you suffered? Alas, perhaps year after
year your suffering remained unchanged, and if it did
change, then its description would be a matter for the
doctor or the pastor. Alas, perhaps the unaltered monotony
of the suffering seems to you like a creeping death. But
while the doctor and the pastor and your friend know
of no change to speak of, yet the talk asks you whether
under the pressure of the unchanged monotony an infinite
change is taking place. Not a change in the suffering (for
even if it is changed, it can only be a finite change), but
in you, an infinite change in you from good to better. If
the talk were to characterize your altered condition
through the years, would it dare use the words of the
Apostle and say of your life of unaltered suffering: "Suffering taught him patience, patience taught him experience, experience taught him hope?"[47] Would the talk dare
say at your grave: "He won that hope that shall never
be put to shame"? At your grave, instead of mumbling
a prayer of thanks that the sufferer is dead as was described
earlier, would the talk dare freely and wholeheartedly to
say, as though at a hero's grave, "The content of his life
was suffering, yet his life has put many to shame"? For
in eternity there will be as little asked about your suffering as about the king's purple, precisely as little. In eter-

nity you as an individual will only be asked about your
faith and about your faithfulness. There will be absolutely
no asking about whether you were entrusted with much
or little, whether you were given many talents of silver
to work with or whether you were given a hundred-pound
weight to carry. But you will be asked only about your
faith and about your faithfulness. In the world of time
one asks in other terms. Here one inquires especially about
how high a command a man has, and when it is a very
high one, then one forgets in one's worldly astonishment
to ask after his faithfulness. But if it is very little, then
one prefers to hear nothing at all about him, neither about
his burden nor his faithfulness. Eternity asks solely about
faithfulness, and with equal earnestness it asks this of
the king and of the most wretched of all sufferers. It is
no excuse to be entrusted with little, nor is it any answer
to the question that asks exclusively about faithfulness,
the question, which in the eternal mercy knows that sufferings can tempt a man, but knows, too, that they can
be a guide. For "sorrow is better than laughter; for by
the sadness of the countenance, the heart is made better"
(Ecclesiastes 7:3). This is the change that eternity asks
about, not about the unchangeableness of the suffering.
This is what eternity asks; and if you yourself actively
consider the occasion of this talk, then you will ask yourself about this matter. If the change has not taken place,
then this question of whether it has truthfully been done
will indeed be helpful to you in bringing about the change.
For human sympathy, no matter how painstakingly it inquires about you, cannot by all its questioning alter the
fixed character of the suffering. Eternity's question, if you
put it truthfully to yourself before God, contains the possibility of change. But I am talking almost as if I meant
to edify you. Yet out of respect for you, the talk would

be embarrassed to press this question upon you. You yourself know best of all, that if you put this question, then
you must render an account of whether you are living
in this way at present.

15. Conclusion:
Man and the Eternal

THIS WAS the issue of the talk. But now if the
individual, yes, if you, my listener, and I must admit to
ourselves that we were far from living in this way, far
from that purity of heart which truthfully wills but one
thing; must admit to ourselves that the questions demanded an answer, and yet in another sense, in order to
avoid any deception, did not require an answer, in that
they were, if anything, charges against ourselves which in
spite of the form of the question changed themselves into
an accusation: then should the individual, and you, my
listener, and I join together in saying, "Indeed our life
is like that of most others"? How, then, shall we begin
over again, at this time, and once more speak of the evasion which consists of being among the many? For where
there are many, there is externality, and comparison, and
indulgence, and excuse and evasion. Shall we, even after
we have come to understand the calamity of this evasion,
in the end take refuge in it? Shall we console ourselves
with a common plight? Alas, even in the world of time,
a common plight is a doubtful consolation; and in eternity there is no common plight. In eternity, the individual,
yes, you, my listener, and I as individuals will each be
asked solely about himself as an individual, and about the

individual details in his life. If in this talk I have spoken
poorly, then you will not be asked about that, my listener;
nor will any man from whom I may have learned. For
if he has stated it falsely, then he will be questioned about
that and I will be made to answer for having learned from
another what was false. Nor will any with whom I have
had an acquaintance be made to answer. For if his acquaintance was corrupting, then he will be questioned
about that, but I shall be made to answer for having
sought out or not having avoided his acquaintance, and
for letting myself become corrupted. No, if I have spoken
poorly and just in so far as I have spoken poorly, then
without any excuse whatsoever I, as an individual, will
be questioned about that. For in eternity there is not the
remotest thought of any common plight. In eternity, the
individual, yes, you, my listener, and I as individuals will
each be asked solely about himself as an individual and
about the individual details in his life.

If it should so happen that in this talk I have spoken
the truth, then I shall be questioned no further about this
matter. There will be no questioning as to whether I have
won men (quite on the contrary, it might well be asked
whether I had any notion of having by my own efforts
done the least thing toward winning them); no questioning as to whether, by the talk I have gained some earthly
advantage (quite on the contrary, it might well be asked
whether I had any notion of having myself done the least
thing toward gaining it); no questioning about what results I have produced, or whether I may have produced
no results at all, or whether loss and the sport that others
made of me were the only results I have produced. No,
eternity will release me from one and all of such foolish
questions. In the world of time a man can be confused,
for he does not know which is which: which question is

the serious one and which the silly one, especially since the silly one is heard a thousand times to the serious question's once. Eternity, on the other hand, can admirably distinguish between them; yet it is obvious that the thing does not become easier on that account. The seriousness of the plight is only intensified. For in eternity there is not the remotest thought of any common plight. In eternity, the individual, yes, you, my listener, and I as individuals will each be asked solely about himself as an individual, and about the individual details in his life. If it should happen that a true reflection of life is contained in this talk, if it is so that the ability and the occasion is vouchsafed me which enabled me to set it forth; yet it may also have happened, we can suppose such a case, that the circumstances under which it had to be spoken did not seem favorable. If this were so, then eternity would not inquisitively enter into any long-drawn-out discourse about circumstances. Had I remained silent, eternity would hold me as an individual to account. For in the world of time, when the task is to be clever for one's own advantage, when worldly cleverness judges and criticizes, then unfavorable circumstances are not only a ground for silence, but silence becomes admired as cleverness; while favorable circumstances are an invitation for all to join in the conversation. On the other hand, in the eternal order, if the circumstances are difficult the obligation to speak is doubled. The difficulty is precisely an invitation. Eternally, the individual will only be asked whether he knew that they were unfavorable, and whether in this event he dared remain silent and therefore by his silence, yes, to use the proverb, by his consent, he had as an individual contributed to a condition where the circumstances became still more unfavorable for the truth. Eternally, circumstances will provide neither hiding place nor evasion for him, for he will be asked as an individual, and the difficulty of the circumstances will stand against him as a double accusation. As for remaining silent, it is not as with sleeping that he who sleeps does not sin. For in the world the individual has brought the most atrocious guilt upon himself—through remaining silent. The fault was not that he did not manage to get the circumstances changed. The fault was that he was silent not out of discretion, which is silent when it is proper to be silent, but out of cleverness, which is silent because it is the most prudent to be so.

But what, then, shall we do, if the questions sound like accusations? Above all else, each one will himself become an individual with his responsibility to God. Each one will himself be subject to the stern judgment of this individuality. Is this not the purpose of the office of Confession? For just as little as in that silent churchyard "the multitude of dead make up a society," so little does the multitude of those coming to confess make up a society —for not even the king goes to confession alone in order to escape the common company of others. Those who are coming to confess do not belong together in a society. Each one is an individual before God. Man and wife may go to confession in beautiful fellowship with each other, but they may not confess together. The one who confesses is not in company, he is as an individual, alone before God. And if, as an individual he admits to himself that the questions, which by the help of an insignificant one's whisper he puts to himself, are accusations, then he confesses. For one does not confess merits and achievements, he confesses sins. When one confesses, he sees at once that he has no merits. He sees that merits and achievements are fantasies and sense deceptions that are at home where one moves about in the crowd and engages others in conversation. He sees that it is just on this account that the one who never himself becomes an individual is easily tempted to consider himself a most meritorious man. But the purpose of the office of Confession is certainly not to make a man conscious of himself as an individual at the moment of its celebration, and then for the rest of the time to allow him to live outside this consciousness. On the contrary, in the moment of confession itself he should give account as to how he has lived as an individual. If the same consciousness were not demanded of him for daily use, then the demand of the office of Confession is a self-contradiction. It is as if one now and then demanded of a humble man that he should render account to himself and to God of how he had lived as a king—he that had never been a king. And so it is to ask of a man that he shall render account of his life as an individual when one allows him to lead his life outside this consciousness.

My listener! Do you remember now, how this talk began? Let me call it back to your remembrance. It is true that the temporal order has its time; but the Eternal shall always have time. If this should not happen within a man's life, then the Eternal comes again under another name, and once again shall always have time. This is repentance. And since at present no man's life is lived in perfection, but each one in frailty, so Providence has given man two companions for his journey, the one calls him forward, the other calls him back. But the call of repentance is always at the eleventh hour. Therefore confession is always at the eleventh hour, but not in the sense of being precipitate. For confession is a holy act, which calls for a collected mind. A collected mind is a mind that has collected itself from every distraction, from every relation, in order to center itself upon this relation to itself as an individual who is responsible to God. It is a mind that has collected itself from every distraction, and therefore also from all comparison. For comparison may either tempt a man to an earthly and fortuitous despondency because the one who compares must admit to himself that he is behind many others, or it may tempt him to pride because, humanly speaking, he seems to be ahead of many others.

A new expression of the true extremity of the eleventh hour comes when the penitent has withdrawn himself from every relation in order to center himself upon his relation to himself as an individual. By this he becomes responsible for every relation in which he ordinarily stands, and he is outside of any comparison. The more use one makes of comparison, the more it seems that there is still plenty of time. The more a man makes use of comparison, the more indolent and the more wretched his life becomes. But when all comparison is relinquished forever then a man confesses as an individual before God—and he is outside any comparison, just as the demand which purity of heart lays upon him is outside of comparison. Purity of heart is what God requires of him and the penitent demands it of himself before God. Yes, it is just on this account that he confesses his sins. And heavy as the way and the hour of the confession may be, yet the penitent wins the Eternal. He is strengthened in the consciousness that he is an individual, and in the task of truthfully willing only one thing. This consciousness is the strait gate and the narrow way. For it is not this narrow way that the many take, following one after another. No, this straitness means rather that each must himself become an individual, that through this needle's eyes he must press forward to the narrow way where no comparison cools, but yet where no comparison kills with its insidious cooling. The broad way, on the other hand, is broad because so many travel upon it. The crowd's way is always broad. There the poisonous ornamental flower of excuses is found in bloom. The inviting hiding places of evasion are there. There comparison wafts its cooling breath of air. This way leadeth not unto life.

Only the individual can truthfully will the Good, and even though the penitent toils heavily not merely in the eleventh hour of confession, with all the questions standing as accusations of himself, but also in their daily use in repentance, yet the way is the right one. For he is in touch with the demand that calls for purity of heart by willing only one thing.

If you, my listener, unquestionably know much more concerning the office of Confession than has been set forth here; if you know the next thing that follows upon the confession of sins, still this extended talk has not been in vain if it has made you pause, made you pause before something that you already know well, you, who know so much more. But do not forget, that the most terrible thing of all is to "live on, deceived, not by what one might expect to be deceived (alas, and on that account horribly deceived) but deceived by too much knowledge." Consider that in these times it is a particularly great temptation for speakers to leave the individual as quickly as possible in order to get as much as possible said, so that nobody might suspect that the speaker did not know what every man in a Christian country knows. Alas, only God knows how the individual knows it. But what does it profit a man if he goes further and further and it must be said of him: he never stops going further; when it also must be said of him: there was nothing that made him pause? For pausing is not a sluggish repose. Pausing is also movement. It is the inward movement of the heart. To pause is to deepen oneself in inwardness. But merely

going further is to go straight in the direction of super-
ficiality. By that way one does not come to will only one
thing. Only if at some time he decisively stopped going
further and then again came to a pause, as he went further, only then could he will only one thing. For purity
of heart was to will one thing.

Father in Heaven! What is a man without Thee! What
is all that he knows, vast accumulation though it be, but
a chipped fragment if he does not know Thee! What is
all his striving, could it even encompass the world, but
a half-finished work if he does not know Thee: Thee the
One, who art one thing and who art all! So may Thou
give to the intellect, wisdom to comprehend that one thing;
to the heart, sincerity to receive this understanding; to
the will, purity that wills only one thing. In prosperity
may Thou grant perseverance to will one thing; amid
distractions, collectedness to will one thing; in suffering,
patience to will one thing. Oh, Thou that giveth both the
beginning and the completion, may Thou early, at the
dawn of day, give to the young man the resolution to
will one thing. As the day wanes, may Thou give to the
old man a renewed remembrance of his first resolution,
that the first may be like the last, the last like the first,
in possession of a life that has willed only one thing.
Alas, but this has indeed not come to pass. Something has
come in between. The separation of sin lies in between.
Each day, and day after day something is being placed
in between: delay, blockage, interruption, delusion, corruption. So in this time of repentance may Thou give
the courage once again to will one thing. True, it is an
interruption of our daily tasks; we do lay down our work
as though it were a day of rest, when the penitent (and
it is only in a time of repentance that the heavy-laden

worker may be quiet in the confession of sin) is alone before Thee in self-accusation. This is indeed an interruption. But it is an interruption that searches back into its very beginnings that it might bind up anew that which sin has separated, that in its grief it might atone for lost time, that in its anxiety it might bring to completion that which lies before it. Oh, Thou that givest both the beginning and the completion, give Thou victory in the day of need so that what neither a man's burning wish nor his determined resolution may attain to, may be granted unto him in the sorrowing of repentance: to will only one thing.

Notes

[1] Ecclesiastes 3:1.

[2] Kierkegaard often takes some liberty with his quotations paraphrasing what he takes them essentially to mean. "He hath made everything beautiful in his time: also he hath set the world in their heart from the beginning to the end."

[3] For example: 2 Thessalonians 1:3.

[4] Matthew 23:23. See note 2. The precise text is: "These ought ye to have done and not to leave the other undone."

[5] James 3:5.

[6] Matthew 12:43, 45.

[7] Compare Börne, *Collected Works*, Vol. II, p. 126: "All are not free who scoff at their chains."

[8] Compare Thrasymachus in Plato's *Republic* I. 16, 20.

[9] Compare Romans 8:38, 39.

[10] 1 John 5:19.

[11] Of Themistocles in Cicero's *de Oratore* II. 74, 299.

[12] Plato's *Republic* IX. 572.

[13] Genesis 2:18.

[14] Ecclesiastes 4:10.

[15] Compare Luke 17:10.

[16] See translator's introduction.

[17] These words are attributed to Francis I as having been spoken after the battle of Pavia where he was taken prisoner.

[18] Compare 2 Timothy 3:7.

[19] Psalms 94:9.

[20] Proverbs 4:23.

[21] Ecclesiastes 7:2.

[22] Compare Luke 9:59.

[23] Compare Luke 17:10.

[24] Compare Mark 8:36.

[25] Matthew 27:41-44.

[26] Shakespeare in *Henry V*, Act 2, Scene 4.

[27] Socrates, Plato's *Republic* VI. 492 B.

[28] John the Baptist.

[29] Compare Rosenkranz, *Erinnerungen an Karl Daub*, p. 24: "So as on sentry duty, at night on a lonely post, perhaps before a powder magazine a man has thoughts that under any other circumstances would be quite impossible."

Kierkegaard refers to this same passage again in *Fear and Trembling, Collected Works*, Vol. III, p. 100.

[30] Genesis 12:1.

[31] Jose Arndt's, *True Christianity*.

[32] Luke 15:7.

[33] Compare Matthew 11:28.

[34] Epicurus in Diogenes Laertius, 140.

[35] Mark 9:36.

[36] Ephesians 6:14, 17.

[37] Acts 5:40-41.

[38] The Danish word for "courage" is *Mod* and for "opposition" is *Modstand*. (Tr.)

[39] The Danish word for "patience," *Taalmod*, contains the Danish word for "courage," *Mod*, and invites the discourse which follows. (Tr.)

[40] Compare Acts 22:27-30, and 24:23.

[41] Compare 1 Peter 1:16.

[42] The Danish word for "actor," *Skuespiller*, means literally *show* or *display—player*. (Tr.)

[43] Socrates in Plato's *Republic* VII. 518 A.

[44] Psalms 2:4.

[45] The Latin proverb "Tu si tacuisses, philosophus mansisses." See Boethius *Consolatio philos.* II. 17.

[46] Proverbs 25:13.

[47] Romans 5:3-4.

American Studies: General

HENRY STEELE COMMAGER, Ed.: The Struggle for Racial Equality   TB/1300
CARL N. DEGLER: Out of Our Past: *The Forces that Shaped Modern America*   CN/2
CARL N. DEGLER, Ed.: Pivotal Interpretations of American History
Vol. I TB/1240;   Vol. II TB/1241
A. S. EISENSTADT, Ed.: The Craft of American History: *Selected Essays*
Vol. I TB/1255;   Vol. II TB/1256
ROBERT L. HEILBRONER: The Limits of American Capitalism   TB/1305
JOHN HIGHAM, Ed.: The Reconstruction of American History   TB/1068
ROBERT H. JACKSON: The Supreme Court in the American System of Government   TB/1106
JOHN F. KENNEDY: A Nation of Immigrants. *Illus. Revised and Enlarged. Introduction by Robert F. Kennedy*   TB/1118
RICHARD B. MORRIS: Fair Trial: *Fourteen Who Stood Accused, from Anne Hutchinson to Alger Hiss*   TB/1335
GUNNAR MYRDAL: An American Dilemma: *The Negro Problem and Modern Democracy. Introduction by the Author.*
Vol. I TB/1443;   Vol. II TB/1444
GILBERT OSOFSKY, Ed.: The Burden of Race: *A Documentary History of Negro-White Relations in America*   TB/1405
ARNOLD ROSE: The Negro in America: *The Condensed Version of Gunnar Myrdal's An American Dilemma. Second Edition* TB/3048
JOHN E. SMITH: Themes in American Philosophy: *Purpose, Experience and Community* TB/1466
WILLIAM R. TAYLOR: Cavalier and Yankee: *The Old South and American National Character* TB/1474

American Studies: Colonial

BERNARD BAILYN: The New England Merchants in the Seventeenth Century   TB/1149
ROBERT E. BROWN: Middle-Class Democracy and Revolution in Massachusetts, 1691–1780. *New Introduction by Author*   TB/1413
JOSEPH CHARLES: The Origins of the American Party System   TB/1049
WESLEY FRANK CRAVEN: The Colonies in Transition: 1660-1712†   TB/3084

CHARLES GIBSON: Spain in America †   TB/3077
CHARLES GIBSON, Ed.: The Spanish Tradition in America +   HR/1351
LAWRENCE HENRY GIPSON: The Coming of the Revolution: 1763-1775. † *Illus.* TB/3007
PERRY MILLER: Errand Into the Wilderness   TB/1139
PERRY MILLER & T. H. JOHNSON, Eds.: The Puritans: *A Sourcebook of Their Writings*
Vol. I TB/1093;   Vol. II TB/1094
EDMUND S. MORGAN: The Puritan Family: *Religion and Domestic Relations in Seventeenth Century New England*   TB/1227
WALLACE NOTESTEIN: The English People on the Eve of Colonization: 1603-1630. † *Illus.*
TB/3006
LOUIS B. WRIGHT: The Cultural Life of the American Colonies: 1607-1763. † *Illus.*
TB/3005

American Studies: The Revolution to 1860

JOHN R. ALDEN: The American Revolution: 1775-1783. † *Illus.*   TB/3011
RAY A. BILLINGTON: The Far Western Frontier: 1830-1860. † *Illus.*   TB/3012
GEORGE DANGERFIELD: The Awakening of American Nationalism, 1815-1828. † *Illus.* TB/3061
CLEMENT EATON: The Growth of Southern Civilization, 1790-1860. † *Illus.*   TB/3040
LOUIS FILLER: The Crusade against Slavery: 1830-1860. † *Illus.*   TB/3029
WILLIM W. FREEHLING: Prelude to Civil War: *The Nullification Controversy in South Carolina, 1816-1836*   TB/1359
THOMAS JEFFERSON: Notes on the State of Virginia. ‡ *Edited by Thomas P. Abernethy*
TB/3052
JOHN C. MILLER: The Federalist Era: 1789-1801. † *Illus.*   TB/3027
RICHARD B. MORRIS: The American Revolution Reconsidered   TB/1363
GILBERT OSOFSKY, Ed.: Puttin' On Ole Massa: *The Slave Narratives of Henry Bibb, William Wells Brown, and Solomon Northup* ‡
TB/1432
FRANCIS S. PHILBRICK: The Rise of the West, 1754-1830. † *Illus.*   TB/3067
MARSHALL SMELSER: The Democratic Republic, 1801-1815 †   TB/1406

† The New American Nation Series, edited by Henry Steele Commager and Richard B. Morris.
‡ American Perspectives series, edited by Bernard Wishy and William E. Leuchtenburg.
α History of Europe series, edited by J. H. Plumb.
§ The Library of Religion and Culture, edited by Benjamin Nelson.
‖ Researches in the Social, Cultural, and Behavioral Sciences, edited by Benjamin Nelson.
≍ Harper Modern Science Series, edited by James A. Newman.
° Not for sale in Canada.
∔ Documentary History of the United States series, edited by Richard B. Morris.
Documentary History of Western Civilization series, edited by Eugene C. Black and Leonard W. Levy.
Λ The Economic History of the United States series, edited by Henry David et al.
¶ European Perspectives series, edited by Eugene C. Black.
** Contemporary Essays series, edited by Leonard W. Levy.
* The Stratum Series, edited by John Hale.

LOUIS B. WRIGHT: Culture on the Moving Frontier   TB/1053

American Studies: The Civil War to 1900

T. C. COCHRAN & WILLIAM MILLER: The Age of Enterprise: *A Social History of Industrial America*   TB/1054
W. A. DUNNING: Reconstruction, Political and Economic: 1865-1877   TB/1073
HAROLD U. FAULKNER: Politics, Reform and Expansion: 1890-1900. † *Illus.*   TB/3020
GEORGE M. FREDRICKSON: The Inner Civil War: *Northern Intellectuals and the Crisis of the Union*   TB/1358
JOHN A. GARRATY: The New Commonwealth, 1877-1890 †   TB/1410
HELEN HUNT JACKSON: A Century of Dishonor: *The Early Crusade for Indian Reform.* † *Edited by Andrew F. Rolle*   TB/3063
WILLIAM G. MCLOUGHLIN, Ed.: The American Evangelicals, 1800-1900: An Anthology ‡   TB/1382
JAMES S. PIKE: The Prostrate State: *South Carolina under Negro Government.* ‡ *Intro. by Robert F. Durden*   TB/3085
VERNON LANE WHARTON: The Negro in Mississippi, 1865-1890   TB/1178

American Studies: The Twentieth Century

RAY STANNARD BAKER: Following the Color Line: *American Negro Citizenship in Progressive Era.* ‡ *Edited by Dewey W. Grantham, Jr. Illus.*   TB/3053
RANDOLPH S. BOURNE: War and the Intellectuals: *Collected Essays, 1915-1919.* ‡ *Edited by Carl Resek*   TB/3043
A. RUSSELL BUCHANAN: The United States and World War II. † *Illus.*
                                Vol. I TB/3044; Vol. II TB/3045
THOMAS C. COCHRAN: The American Business System: *A Historical Perspective, 1900-1955*   TB/1080
FOSTER RHEA DULLES: America's Rise to World Power: 1898-1954. † *Illus.*   TB/3021
HAROLD U. FAULKNER: The Decline of Laissez Faire, 1897-1917   TB/1397
JOHN D. HICKS: Republican Ascendancy: 1921-1933. † *Illus.*   TB/3041
WILLIAM E. LEUCHTENBURG: Franklin D. Roosevelt and the New Deal: 1932-1940. † *Illus.*   TB/3025
WILLIAM E. LEUCHTENBURG, Ed.: The New Deal: *A Documentary History* +   HR/1354
ARTHUR S. LINK: Woodrow Wilson and the Progressive Era: 1910-1917. † *Illus.*   TB/3023
BROADUS MITCHELL: Depression Decade: *From New Era through New Deal, 1929-1941* ∆   TB/1439
GEORGE E. MOWRY: The Era of Theodore Roosevelt and the Birth of Modern America: 1900-1912. † *Illus.*   TB/3022
WILLIAM PRESTON, JR.: Aliens and Dissenters:
TWELVE SOUTHERNERS: I'll Take My Stand: *The South and the Agrarian Tradition. Intro. by Louis D. Rubin, Jr.; Biographical Essays by Virginia Rock*   TB/1072

Art, Art History, Aesthetics

ERWIN PANOFSKY: Renaissance and Renascences in Western Art. *Illus.*   TB/1447
ERWIN PANOFSKY: Studies in Iconology: *Humanistic Themes in the Art of the Renaissance. 180 illus.*   TB/1077
HEINRICH ZIMMER: Myths and Symbols in Indian Art and Civilization. *70 illus.*   TB/2005

Asian Studies

WOLFGANG FRANKE: China and the West: *The Cultural Encounter, 13th to 20th Centuries. Trans. by R. A. Wilson*   TB/1326
L. CARRINGTON GOODRICH: A Short History of the Chinese People. *Illus.*   TB/3015

Economics & Economic History

C. E. BLACK: The Dynamics of Modernization: *A Study in Comparative History*   TB/1321
GILBERT BURCK & EDITORS OF Fortune: The Computer Age: *And its Potential for Management*   TB/1179
ROBERT L. HEILBRONER: The Future as History: *The Historic Currents of Our Time and the Direction in Which They Are Taking America*   TB/1386
ROBERT L. HEILBRONER: The Great Ascent: *The Struggle for Economic Development in Our Time*   TB/3030
FRANK H. KNIGHT: The Economic Organization   TB/1214
DAVID S. LANDES: Bankers and Pashas: *International Finance and Economic Imperialism in Egypt. New Preface by the Author*   TB/1412
ROBERT LATOUCHE: The Birth of Western Economy: *Economic Aspects of the Dark Ages* TB/1290
W. ARTHUR LEWIS: The Principles of Economic Planning. *New Introduction by the Author°*   TB/1436
WILLIAM MILLER, Ed.: Men in Business: *Essays on the Historical Role of the Entrepreneur*   TB/1081
HERBERT A. SIMON: The Shape of Automation: *For Men and Management*   TB/1245

Historiography and History of Ideas

J. BRONOWSKI & BRUCE MAZLISH: The Western Intellectual Tradition: *From Leonardo to Hegel*   TB/3001
WILHELM DILTHEY: Pattern and Meaning in History: *Thoughts on History and Society.° Edited with an Intro. by H. P. Rickman*   TB/1075
J. H. HEXTER: More's Utopia: *The Biography of an Idea. Epilogue by the Author*   TB/1195
H. STUART HUGHES: History as Art and as Science: *Twin Vistas on the Past*   TB/1207
ARTHUR O. LOVEJOY: The Great Chain of Being: *A Study of the History of an Idea*   TB/1009
RICHARD H. POPKIN: The History of Scepticism from Erasmus to Descartes. *Revised Edition*   TB/1391
BRUNO SNELL: The Discovery of the Mind: *The Greek Origins of European Thought*   TB/1018

History: General

HANS KOHN: The Age of Nationalism: *The First Era of Global History*   TB/1380
BERNARD LEWIS: The Arabs in History   TB/1029
BERNARD LEWIS: The Middle East and the West °   TB/1274

History: Ancient

A. ANDREWS: The Greek Tyrants   TB/1103
THEODOR H. GASTER: Thespis: *Ritual Myth and Drama in the Ancient Near East*   TB/1281

2

3

Vol. II: Renaissance, Enlightenment, Modern
TB/39
LUDWIG WITTGENSTEIN: The Blue and Brown
Books °   TB/1211
LUDWIG WITTGENSTEIN: Notebooks, 1914-1916
TB/1441

Political Science & Government

C. E. BLACK: The Dynamics of Modernization:
A Study in Comparative History   TB/1321
DENIS W. BROGAN: Politics in America. *New
Introduction by the Author*   TB/1469
ROBERT CONQUEST: Power and Policy in the
USSR: *The Study of Soviet Dynastics* °
TB/1307
JOHN B. MORRALL: Political Thought in Medieval
Times   TB/1076
KARL R. POPPER: The Open Society and Its
Enemies *Vol. I: The Spell of Plato* TB/1101
*Vol. II: The High Tide of Prophecy: Hegel,
Marx, and the Aftermath*   TB/1102
HENRI DE SAINT-SIMON: Social Organization, The
Science of Man, and Other Writings. ||
*Edited and Translated with an Introduction
by Felix Markham*   TB/1152
CHARLES SCHOTTLAND, Ed.: The Welfare State **
TB/1323
JOSEPH A. SCHUMPETER: Capitalism, Socialism
and Democracy   TB/3008

Psychology

LUDWIG BINSWANGER: Being-in-the-World: *Se-
lected Papers.* || *Trans. with Intro. by Jacob
Needleman*   TB/1365
MIRCEA ELIADE: Cosmos and History: *The Myth
of the Eternal Return* §   TB/2050
MIRCEA ELIADE: Myth and Reality   TB/1369
SIGMUND FREUD: On Creativity and the Uncon-
scious: *Papers on the Psychology of Art,
Literature, Love, Religion.* § *Intro. by Ben-
jamin Nelson*   TB/45
J. GLENN GRAY: The Warriors: *Reflections on
Men in Battle. Introduction by Hannah
Arendt*   TB/1294
WILLIAM JAMES: Psychology: *The Briefer
Course. Edited with an Intro. by Gordon
Allport*   TB/1034

*Religion: Ancient and Classical, Biblical and
Judaic Traditions*

MARTIN BUBER: Eclipse of God: *Studies in the
Relation Between Religion and Philosophy*
TB/12
MARTIN BUBER: Hasidism and Modern Man.
Edited and Translated by Maurice Friedman
TB/839
MARTIN BUBER: The Knowledge of Man. *Edited
with an Introduction by Maurice Friedman.
Translated by Maurice Friedman and Ronald
Gregor Smith*   TB/135
MARTIN BUBER: Moses. *The Revelation and the
Covenant*   TB/837
MARTIN BUBER: The Origin and Meaning of
Hasidism. *Edited and Translated by Maurice
Friedman*   TB/835
MARTIN BUBER: The Prophetic Faith TB/73
MARTIN BUBER: Two Types of Faith: *Interpene-
tration of Judaism and Christianity* ° TB/75
M. S. ENSLIN: Christian Beginnings TB/5
M. S. ENSLIN: The Literature of the Christian
Movement   TB/6
HENRI FRANKFORT: Ancient Egyptian Religion:
An Interpretation   TB/77

*Religion: Early Christianity Through
Reformation*

ANSELM OF CANTERBURY: Truth, Freedom, and
Evil: *Three Philosophical Dialogues. Edited
and Translated by Jasper Hopkins and Herbert Richardson*   TB/317
EDGAR J. GOODSPEED: A Life of Jesus TB/1
ROBERT M. GRANT: Gnosticism and Early Christianity   TB/136

Religion: Oriental Religions

TOR ANDRAE: Mohammed: *The Man and His
Faith* §   TB/62
EDWARD CONZE: Buddhism: *Its Essence and De-
velopment.* ° *Foreword by Arthur Waley*
TB/58
H. G. CREEL: Confucius and the Chinese Way
TB/63
FRANKLIN EDGERTON, Trans. & Ed.: The Bhaga-
vad Gita   TB/115
SWAMI NIKHILANANDA, Trans. & Ed.: The
Upanishads   TB/114
D. T. SUZUKI: On Indian Mahayana Buddhism.
° *Ed. with Intro. by Edward Conze.* TB/1403

Science and Mathematics

W. E. LE GROS CLARK: The Antecedents of
Man: *An Introduction to the Evolution of
the Primates.* ° *Illus.*   TB/559
ROBERT E. COKER: Streams, Lakes, Ponds. *Illus.*
TB/586
ROBERT E. COKER: This Great and Wide Sea: *An
Introduction to Oceanography and Marine
Biology. Illus.*   TB/551
WILLARD VAN ORMAN QUINE: Mathematical Logic
TB/558

Sociology and Anthropology

REINHARD BENDIX: Work and Authority in In-
dustry: *Ideologies of Management in the
Course of Industrialization*   TB/3035
KENNETH B. CLARK: Dark Ghetto: *Dilemmas of
Social Power. Foreword by Gunnar Myrdal*
TB/1317
KENNETH CLARK & JEANNETTE HOPKINS: A Rele-
vant War Against Poverty: *A Study of Com-
munity Action Programs and Observable So-
cial Change*   TB/1480
LEWIS COSER, Ed.: Political Sociology TB/1293
GARY T. MARX: Protest and Prejudice: *A Study
of Belief in the Black Community* TB/1435
ROBERT K. MERTON, LEONARD BROOM, LEONARD S.
COTTRELL, JR., Editors: Sociology Today:
Problems and Prospects ||
Vol. I TB/1173; Vol. II TB/1174
GILBERT OSOFSKY, Ed.: The Burden of Race: *A
Documentary History of Negro-White Rela-
tions in America*   TB/1405
GILBERT OSOFSKY: Harlem: The Making of a
Ghetto: *Negro New York 1890-1930* TB/1381
PHILIP RIEFF: The Triumph of the Therapeutic:
Uses of Faith After Freud   TB/1360
ARNOLD ROSE: The Negro in America: *The Con-
densed Version of Gunnar Myrdal's* An
American Dilemma. *Second Edition* TB/3048
GEORGE ROSEN: Madness in Society: *Chapters in
the Historical Sociology of Mental Illness.* ||
Preface by Benjamin Nelson   TB/1337
PITIRIM A. SOROKIN: Contemporary Sociological
Theories: *Through the First Quarter of the
Twentieth Century*   TB/3046
FLORIAN ZNANIECKI: The Social Role of the
Man of Knowledge. *Introduction by Lewis
A. Coser*   TB/1372

4